Lexington Historical Society

Papers Relating to the History of the Town

Vol. I

Lexington Historical Society

Papers Relating to the History of the Town
Vol. I

ISBN/EAN: 9783337221423

Hergestellt in Europa, USA, Kanada, Australien, Japan

Cover: Foto ©ninafisch / pixelio.de

Weitere Bücher finden Sie auf **www.hansebooks.com**

LEXINGTON

HISTORICAL SOCIETY

PAPERS RELATING TO THE

HISTORY OF THE TOWN

READ BY SOME OF THE MEMBERS

VOL. I.

LEXINGTON MASS.
PUBLISHED BY THE HISTORICAL SOCIETY
1889

CONTENTS.

Origin of the Name "Lexington,"	9
A Sketch of the History of Lexington Common, . .	17
Robert Munroe, ...	38
Captain John Parker, ...	42
A Few Words for our Grandmothers of 1775, . . .	48
Matthew Bridge, ...	54
Reminiscences of a Participant in the Occurrences of April 19, 1775, ...	59
Amos Locke, ...	67
The Old Taverns of Lexington, ...	73
Lexington Academy, ...	88
Lexington Normal School, ...	95
A Sketch of the Life and Character of the Late William Eustis, ...	101
Colonel Francis Faulkner and the Battle of Lexington, ...	110
Lexington in 1775 and in 1861, ...	117
Appendix:	
The Second Meeting-house in Lexington, ...	129
Some Facts relating to the Third Meeting-house in Lexington,	130
List of Pew Owners in the Third Church, ...	134

LEXINGTON HISTORICAL SOCIETY was organized on Tuesday evening, March 16, 1886, for the purpose of local historical research, and of gathering up and preserving such facts and traditions relating to the town as may be deemed important. Its officers consist of a president, vice-president, secretary, treasurer, historian, custodian, a council, and a committee on publications. Meetings are held on the second Tuesday of October, December, February, March, and April, when papers are read, followed by discussions. The membership includes both men and women, and now numbers about two hundred. Under the following vote, the first volume of papers is now printed.

At a meeting of Lexington Historical Society, held March 12, 1889, the following report of the Council was unanimously adopted : —

1. The Council recommend that a committee of three persons, to be called the Committee on Publications, be chosen, whose duty it shall be to make such selection of papers read before the Society for publication as they may deem advisable, and that the Committee be authorized to make such arrangement and emendation of those selected as will in their judgment best promote historic knowledge and accuracy, and publish them in such form as they may think desirable.

2. That, in the selection and printing of papers, they shall be limited to those which relate to our own town and to the families identified with its history, and especially to such important facts and knowledge as are likely to be lost, if not so gathered up and preserved; that, leaving all matters which have been already treated by historical writers, they shall publish only those papers which elucidate Lexington life and history during

the two and a half centuries since the original settlement of the town.

3. The Council also recommend that the following persons constitute this Committee; namely, Rev. Carlton A. Staples, Rev. Edward G. Porter, and Mrs. Theodore Robinson.

LEXINGTON, Oct. 4, 1889.

ORIGIN OF THE NAME "LEXINGTON."

READ AT THE MEETING OF THE SOCIETY, MAY 13, 1886, BY
A. E. SCOTT.

THE origin of names of cities, towns, and other political divisions is an interesting study. Taking our own State for illustration, we find many names evidently merely descriptive of situation, as the different "fields,"— Westfield, Marshfield, Brookfield, Medfield (Meadfield); or the "fords," like Westford, Medford (Meadford); or like Norton (North town) or Weston (West town). Others are descriptive of physical features, as Watertown, Stoneham, Roxbury (Rocksbury), Marblehead. Occasionally, a typical name is adopted, indicative, perhaps, of the peaceful nature of the region or the character of the people, as Concord, Contentment, the original name of Dedham, or Hopedale, or a Scriptural name, like Salem or Sharon. A few Indian names are retained,— I think it is to be regretted that the number is so small,— as Cohasset, Scituate, Natick.

Many names were adopted, no doubt, in honor of English statesmen, like Leicester (for the Earl of Leicester), Bedford (Duke of Bedford), and Walpole; and some in honor of distinguished men at home, like Harvard, from Rev. John Harvard, the founder of Harvard College. Many names of prominent counties or towns in England were retained by the colonists, like Worcester and Lancaster, the latter taking us back to the Roman *castra*, or camp, on the river Lune.

But by far the greater number of towns in Massachusetts received their names from smaller villages and obscure places in the "mother country," from which the early settlers came or with which their families were associated. These names were given not in accordance with any general plan or system, except that, perhaps, changes in feeling on the part of the colonists toward England or the affiliations and tastes of men in authority had their influence at certain periods on particular classes of names.

Of the names given to the later towns, Arlington, no doubt, was selected because, at the time it was substituted for West Cambridge, the name was somewhat prominently before the country. Physical features of the localities perhaps suggested Belmont and Rockland. Norfolk took the name of its county, Everett the name of the orator; while Wakefield, Maynard, Hudson, Ayer, and Bourne were named from individuals or families more or less prominent in their history or industries. For the same reason, South Abington has just adopted the name of Whitman, and West Medford desires to become Brooks.

Similar processes have been going on in the settlement of the great West. We find scattered through its whole extent counties and towns named from prominent men of our own land, from the features of the localities, from national events, and from the Eastern towns and villages from whence some of the settlers emigrated. The names of all our Presidents have been a fruitful source to draw from, the number of each being somewhat indicative of the esteem in which their names or their virtues are held. The character and struggles of the first settlers of Kansas, no doubt, suggested the names of Lawrence, Franklin, Liberty, Washington, Jefferson, Jackson, Madison, and Independence. The War for the Union has furnished to many towns and villages in the Far West such names as Grant, Logan, Sherman, Sheridan, Lincoln, and Stanton; while many names — such as Prairie Dog, Kill Creek, Driftwood, Tombstone, Yellow Medicine, Fair Play, Skull Valley, You Bet, etc.— of places that have sprung up in regions settled by reckless adventurers reflect the original character and tone of the people.

Perhaps no small town has been more frequently honored by the adoption of its name than Lexington. Soon after the event that made our town famous, the news reached a party of explorers who had encamped on the spot where now stands the beautiful city of Lexington, Ky. Professor Ranck, in an interesting account of the settlement, says: "Delighted with the virgin charms surrounding them, they resolved to make the site of our city their place of settlement, and then and there named it Lexington, in honor of that glorious field where the rebels of Massachusetts had died but a few weeks before, resisting the encroachments of their king."

Here, in the heart of a Virginia wilderness and by Kentucky pioneers, was erected the first monument ever raised on this continent to the first dead of the American Revolution.

Other Lexingtons followed; and to-day we find the name given to county, town, village, or station twenty-four times at least in the following States: South Carolina, Alabama, Georgia, Illinois, Indiana, Iowa, Kansas, Kentucky, Maine, Virginia, Michigan, Minnesota, Mississippi, Missouri, New York, North Carolina, Ohio, Tennessee, Texas.

When I began to study the origin of the name, I was not aware of the discussion that had taken place in regard to it. I naturally turned to English sources of inquiry. Judge of my surprise to find in the Encyclopædia Britannica the only Lexington mentioned was Lexington, Ky. Chambers gives it a bare mention as the scene of the first conflict between the Americans and the British troops in the War for Independence. Other English works of reference were significantly silent.

Turning to the History of Lexington, I found at page 422 that Mr. Hudson, with his usual care, had presented a very interesting theory, claiming that it was the custom in those days, when a town was incorporated, for the act to be passed with a blank for the name, to be filled in by the governor. Joseph Dudley was at that time Governor of the Province, and allied to the Sutton family, one of whom, Robert Sutton, being raised to the peerage, had taken the name of Lord Lexington, and at this time was at the height of his popularity. Mr. Hudson claims that the name was given or suggested by the then governor as a compliment to himself and to his friend and relative.

Soon after the history was published, a carefully prepared paper was presented to the Massachusetts Historical Society by a member (Mr. W. H. Whitmore), in which he took issue with Mr. Hudson, claiming,—first, that there was no proof that Governor Dudley was related or acquainted with Lord Lexington; second, that Governor Dudley had nothing to do with naming the town, that the practice to which Mr. Hudson referred began with Governor Barnard in 1732. He further claims that it was not the custom of the legislature at that period to honor living Englishmen, that Lord Lexington was not pre-eminent, that he was a high Tory, and that the choice would not in any event have fallen on him. Relying on the fact that the early settlers gave to their new homes in many instances the names of the villages whence they emigrated, the writer urges that it is more probable that the name was suggested by the English home of one of the settlers of this precinct. Lexington was incorporated in 1713, but it was set off as a precinct in 1691. In support of his theory, the writer states that the parish records of Laxton, England, show that, forty-two years before, there died there one Francis Whitmore, and that there was living at the same time in that part of Cambridge which was afterward called Lexington another Francis Whitmore, shown by the order fixing the boundary, the line running "on the south side of Francis Whitmore's house towards the town of Cambridge aforesaid."

It is, perhaps, a suggestive coincidence that two Francis Whitmores should be living in these two places at about the same time; but it must be remembered that Lexington was not incorporated for over sixty years after this time, and probably nearly twenty years after the decease of the Cambridge person of that name. And it is certainly strange that no mention or even hint of Lexington is found in any records of this family or precinct until it was inserted in the Act of Incorporation. So that the theory that Lexington, Mass., was named directly after Laxton, England, although very ably advanced, is open, I think, to quite as serious question as the theory of Mr. Hudson that it was named directly from Lord Lexington.

Soon after the publication of the paper above referred

to, there appeared in the *Herald and Genealogist*, a London periodical, a very favorable notice of the paper, but a critical review of the arguments and conclusions. The writer claims that, when the Whitmores lived at Laxton, its former name Lexington was forgotten or disused; but, when our town was named in 1712-13, it had been revived in the creation of the new Lord Lexington, which subsisted until 1723; and, while it is not certain that Governor Dudley was related to the Suttons, there are indications that he was desirous of being so considered; that there is little doubt that Leicester was named by him in 1713-14, after the Earl of Leicester, whose lands adjoined his own in England. Why should he not, then, name Lexington in 1712 and Sutton in 1715 after an English lord, who was certainly somewhat prominent at the time, and with whom he might well desire to be thought to have family connections?

Although we are left by this interesting discussion in some doubt as to the direct origin of the name as applied to our town, the primary source seems undisputed; and, aside from the benefit to be derived from the research and discussion, it seems to be of little moment whether the name comes from Lord Lexington or from Laxton, the manor from whence the title sprang.

Laxton is now an obscure parish in Nottinghamshire; but, in the time of Henry III., it was of considerable importance. In an old book, a copy of which is in the Boston Public Library, entitled "Thoroton's Antiquities of Nottinghamshire," I find the name to be variously spelled Lexington and Lessington,— possibly the former being a euphonic contraction of the latter,— Lexinton (without the "g"), then Laxington, Laxinton, and finally Lexton and Laxton.

The original Lord Lexington was a prominent judge in the reign of Henry III. He was also noted for his great piety and for his ecclesiastical charities. He died in 1250, without offspring. One of his sisters, Alicia, married Robert de Sutton, from whom sprang, after several generations, the last Lord Lexington, to whom we have made frequent reference.

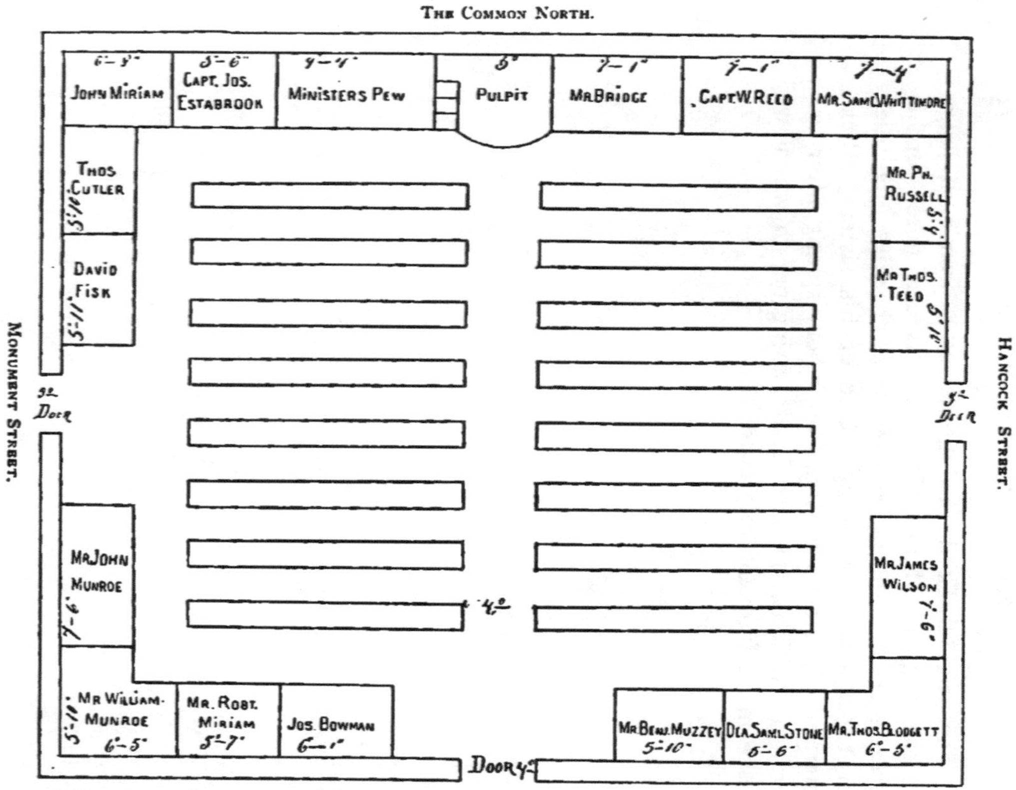
The Common North.
Monument Street.
Hancock Street.
6–9
John Miriam
5–6
Capt. Jos. Estabrook
9–4
Ministers Pew
5
Pulpit
7–1
Mr. Bridge
7–1
Capt. W. Reed
7–4
Mr. Saml Whittimore
Thos Cutler
David Fisk
Mr. Ph. Russell
5:4
Mr. Thos. Teed
5' 10
32 Door
Door
Mr. John Munroe
7–6
Mr. James Wilson
7–6
4
Mr. William Munroe
6–5
Mr. Robt. Miriam
5–7
Jos. Bowman
6–1
Door 4
Mr. Benj. Muzzey
5–10
Dea. Saml. Stone
6–6
Mr. Thos. Blodgett
6–5

A Plan of the Interior of the Second Meeting-house of Lexington, erected by the Town in 1714. The Pews were built by Individuals to whom the Town sold the Spaces, the Size of which is indicated by the Figures on the Plan. The Long Benches were for the People not owning Pews, who were seated according to Age and Property by a Committee chosen for that Purpose. This was the Meeting-house of the

A SKETCH OF THE HISTORY OF LEXINGTON COMMON.

READ OCT. 12, 1886, BY C. A. STAPLES.

On the 6th of January, 1707, one hundred and eighty years ago, a public meeting was held at Cambridge Farms, now Lexington, to consider the buying of a certain piece of land for a common. A committee was chosen, as the records state, to treat with "Nibour Muzzy" about the purchase of a parcel of land lying northward of the meeting-house. Four years and a half pass away, and on June 7, 1711, the committee succeed in accomplishing their object. "Nibour Muzzy" deeds to the inhabitants of the most northerly precinct of Cambridge, commonly called "Cambridge Farms," "a certain parcel of land by estimation one acre and a half, be the same more or less, nigh the meeting-house and bounded northerly by the said Muzzy as the fence now stands, and on the other lines by highways; to have and to hold with all the timber, stones, trees, wood and underwood, herbage and messuage, with all and singular the profits, privileges, and appurtenances thereto belonging."

This was the beginning of Lexington Common. It was bought by subscription. The sum which Muzzy acknowledges to have been paid for this land was £16; but, as the subscription paper containing the names and the sum given by each only amounts to a little over £14, it is possible that no more was raised, and that the balance was donated by Mr. Muzzy. This list of subscribers, entered in full upon our records, is curious and valuable. It contains fifty-two names, and probably indicates the relative wealth of the people living here at that time. Seventeen of the names are represented in Lexington now by their descendants or others bearing them; namely, Estabrooks, Muzzy, Bridge, Stone, Merriam, Locke, Russell, Munroe, Winship, Cutler, Fiske, Stearns, Simonds, Blodget, Brown, Hunt, and Reed. Forty persons on this list, out of fifty-two, are included in these seventeen names; and only eleven or twelve are not now represented here. It shows a permanence of families quite remarkable through these one hundred and eighty years.

On the 1st of February, 1722, the town of Lexington bought of Benjamin and John Muzzy one acre of land as an addition to the Common. In the deed, it is bounded easterly 6¾ rods on a highway leading from Mr. Hancock's to the meeting-house (now Hancock Street), southerly on the Common 28 rods, south-westerly on Concord road 8½ rods, and north-westerly on land of said John and Benjamin Muzzy to a heap of stones at the east corner, near where Hancock Church now stands. For this acre the town pays £25. Benjamin Muzzy is spoken of as a husbandman, and John, as an innholder. The meeting-house referred to in the deed was the first one erected here, and stood a little below the meeting-house monument, recently placed at the southern extremity of the Common,— probably about half-way between that and the watering-trough. It was built in 1692; but what it was like in external appearance no mortal can tell.

Benjamin Muzzy, who sold the Common to the inhabitants of Cambridge Farms, came to this place in 1693.

He owned the land now known as the Merriam place; and his farm included the estates on the north side of the Common,— that of Hancock Church, the Gould, the Swan, and the Simon Robinson places, then having no houses on them, but enclosed and cultivated as a part of his farm. I suppose that he kept a public house, a use to which the place was devoted by himself, and subsequently by his son John, and Messrs. Buckman and Merriam, for a period of nearly one hundred and fifty years. Evidently, he was willing to turn his hand to anything whereby an honest penny could be made; for we find him employed "to ring the bell on Sabbaths, at burials, and on Lecture days — sweep the meeting-house, keep the basin and bring the water for baptising," for all of which he received the sum of £1 15s. per annum.

The first use made of the Common was to build a new meeting-house upon it, in 1713; and in the same year stocks were made, and doubtless placed near it,— a terror to sinners outside and to sleepers inside. Much use seems to have been made of them, since another pair was built a few years afterwards. It would be interesting to know whose ancestors of the present inhabitants of Lexington were sentenced to stand in the stocks, and be hooted at and pelted by the boys. But, happily for their peace of mind, no record of these transactions has been preserved.

The new meeting-house stood on the land lately purchased of "Nibour Muzzy." The front, facing down Main Street, is probably indicated very nearly by the position of the monument there. The building was fifty feet in length by forty feet in width, and twenty-eight feet in height, with three tiers of windows, and with two galleries, one above the other, but with no steeple. It cost nearly

£500, and was finished with pews on the floor, made against the walls, and the interior space filled in with benches. These pews were built by individuals who bought the space for them of the town. In the first book of records, the exact location of each family's pew is described. The edifice belonged to the town, and, as well as the expenses of worship, was paid for by a town tax. The assignment of seats on the benches was made by a committee chosen by the town, who were instructed "to have respect first for age, second for real and personal estate, third to have respect to but one head in a family, and to place the children where they may be inspected." The selectmen order that husband and wife shall sit together with their family if there be room convenient. The pulpit and the front gallery with the pillars were colored; but what color no man knoweth. The town clerk has left this record: "Oct. 17, 1714, was the first Sabbath day we mette in the new meeting-house." It was to be swept "once a fortnight, or equivalent." Here we have the meeting-house of the 19th of April, 1775. It was a square, boxlike building, fronting down Main Street, with an outside door in the centre, and opposite it was the pulpit. There was an outside door, also, in each end. The record shows this conclusively, and proves, also, that the representation of the meeting-house in the Doolittle picture of the battle is substantially true.

Around this meeting-house poured the British soldiers on the morning of the 19th of April, 1775,—a brigade of six hundred splendidly equipped and disciplined men confronting a company of seventy untrained farmers, drawn up there to protect their homes and defend their rights. In the afternoon, the meeting-house was perforated by a ball from Percy's cannon used to cover the British retreat; and it cost £1 1s. to repair the breach.

There was no bell attached to the meeting-house; but a bell was hung on what is called a "Turriott," and was probably the bell that belonged to the previous edifice, given to the town by Cambridge. This building was torn down in 1794 to give place to a more pretentious, comfortable, and beautiful structure, apparently without the slightest hesitation from any feeling of respect for the venerable and historic house. Governor Hancock was foremost in urging its destruction, donating $100 to the town if they would erect a new house of worship. Here the bodies of the dead were brought and laid upon the floor after the battle; and within its walls were gathered the little bands that went forth from time to time in the great struggle for independence, to invoke the blessing of God on the cause to which they dedicated their lives. But the fathers thought it good for nothing but kindling-wood! Such was the beginning and end of the meeting-house of 1714.

The next use made of the Common was in the following year, 1715, when the first school-house in Lexington was built, a picture of which as sketched by Mrs. Gardner Babcock from ths records appears as the frontispiece of this volume, and the first public school was established. That was an important vote passed by the town, Aug. 29, 1715, "That the town will have a school"; and a committee was accordingly chosen to provide "a schoolmaster that will answer the law." In November of the previous year, the town had voted "to eract a school-house 28 ft. long, 20 ft. wide, and 8 or 9 ft. stud," and to place it on the land lately bought of "Nibour Muzzy," and that it be finished by the 1st of October, 1715. Captain Joseph Estabrook is employed as the first teacher, and receives £15 for five months' service, beginning in October and continuing until March. For several years he was retained in this position, the leader in a long line of men and women who have carried on the work of education in this town, among whom are many that have become distinguished as teachers, lawyers, ministers, and men of literature and science. Joseph Estabrook was a brother of the first minister of Lexington, Rev. Benjamin Estabrook, and a son of Rev. Joseph Estabrook, of Concord. He occupied a prominent position in the town, and was evidently much trusted in the management of public affairs. This was not, however, a free school. The town voted that "each scholar that comes to it shall pay two pens per week for reading, and three pens a week for righting and siphering — and what that amounts to at a year's end, so much to be deducted out of the schoolmaster's salary and stopped in the town treasury, for the next year." Shrewd and careful men were the town fathers in those days. The school-house here was the only one in Lexington for a period of eighty years, but schools taught by women were kept in different parts of the town in private houses. It was a low building, finished in one room, and furnished with benches and tables for the scholars, "a great chare" for the master, and an hour-glass. At first, girls were not allowed to attend it, but afterwards it was voted that "gairls" should be received into the school. Town-meetings were sometimes held in the school-house, especially in cold weather, when it was difficult to keep warm in the meeting-house. It was provided with a great open fireplace at one end, as we learn from the frequent bills paid for repairing the chimney, and the fact that two feet of wood were required of each scholar, to keep the fire burning. At the other end was a turret built up on the outside, in which was hung the meeting-house bell. From these particulars we are able to reproduce the original school-house in our frontispiece, and show how it appeared a hundred and seventy-five years ago.

After standing forty-seven years, in 1761 it was sold, and a new one erected where it stood, — a much smaller building, being only twenty feet square and six and one-half feet between joints. It cost £43 13s. 6d. 1qr. While it was building, the school was kept in Widow Harrington's house, who was paid 5s. 6d. for rent. This school-house must have been standing on the Common at the time of the battle, but it is not shown in Doolittle's picture. It remained there until 1797, when it was sold to Matthew Kelley for $48.50. In this year, three school-houses were built in the town, — namely, in the East, South-west, and North Districts; and the scholars of the centre were to be accommodated in them.

On May 1, 1797, the town voted to erect the monument on School-house Hill. This is the old monument standing on the Common to-day. It was erected in 1799 on "School-house Hill"; and this fact proves conclusively that it was a natural elevation, called School-house Hill because the first two school-houses stood there. The mound, therefore, on which the monument stands was not of man's building, but Nature's work, shaped by the hand of man after the second school-house had been removed. The grading of the place was done by the voluntary labor of the townspeople, the town paying for their food and drink while they were doing it. It would have been a great undertaking to raise such a mound by filling in stones and earth, and we may be sure that $19.62, paid Tavern-keeper Dudley for drink and victuals, "furnished when fixing the ground for the monument," as the record says, would have been wholly insufficient.

The building of the monument was a great event in the history of the Common; but our records tell us nothing more than what has been already given, except that it was completed, or the last stone put in place, on July 4, 1799, and that the town paid a bill of $87.63 for cordage to raise it, which was sold again for $49.30. But we may be perfectly sure that the 4th of July, 1799, was a noisy day on Lexington Common and that much New England rum was disposed of at the taverns. $50 was appropriated to cover these expenses.

But to return to the history of the school-houses. We have seen that in 1797 the old one was sold and removed, to make a place for the monument. For the next seven years there was no school-house in this village; but one was located on Mason's Hill, a little below the old Munroe Tavern, to accommodate this and the east village. But in 1804 another school-house — the third — was built on the Common. It was twenty-eight feet by twenty-three feet, and stood forty feet north of the monument toward Elm Avenue, the front being on a line with the rear of the monument. It had a square roof coming to a point in the centre. Several persons now living well remember this building, and attended school in it, Rev. Artemas Muzzey and Mr. William Locke among the number. In 1821, after standing there seventeen years, it was removed to the vicinity of Vine Brook. An important fact in connection with the school must not be omitted; namely, the well dug and stoned in 1734, supplied with a curb and sweep, for the use of the school and the "town people on Sabbath days to drink at." It cost £5 19s. When it was filled up the records say not, and the oldest inhabitant does not remember it; but some traces of it were discovered in the recent improvement of the Common about half-way between the old monument and the flag-staff.

But let us pass to another chapter of this history,—the building of a belfry for a new bell. The account of this affair is curious and interesting. At a town-meeting held in June, 1761, Isaac Stone, as the record says, "came into ye meeting and gave ye town a bell to be for ye town's use forever; which bell was there, and weighed 463 lbs.—and ye moderator in the name of ye town gave him thanks." Immediately it was voted to hang "ye bell on ye top of ye hill, north of Lt. Jonas Munroe's house," and to build a belfry for it, taking the timber from the ministerial land. Accordingly, it was built on the top of what is now known as Belfry Hill, costing £23 7s. 6d. 2far., and the new bell hung there. This was the famous bell which rung the alarm on the morning of the 19th of April, 1775, whose tongue we have among the precious relics in Cary Library. But the new belfry was not allowed to remain long in peace. Lieutenant Jonas Munroe seems to have been a sharp man, with an eye for the main chance. Here was an opportunity to get an income from the fourteen feet square of barren rock on which the belfry stood; and accordingly he demanded rent of the town for that piece of primitive granite. But the article in the town warrant which contained the demand, " passed in the negative." At the next town-meeting he renewed the demand, with the alternative of pay or leave. The town voted to leave. Accordingly, in 1767, a committee was appointed to move it down and place it " where Will Munroe's shop formerly stood at the end of the stables, near the country road." The site chosen for it was on the west side of Monument Street, probably on Mr. Hudson's or Mr. Ham's grounds. But some people were much opposed to its standing there; and it seems to have been moved, probably in the night, across the street on to the Common. Immediately a town-meeting was called, to take action upon the matter. There were four articles in the town warrant regarding the belfry: 1. "To see if ye town cannot agree to and pitch upon some place for ye bell and belfry to stand for ye future, and confirm it by a vote that may have a tendency to make peace in ye town and better accommodate ye whole town than where it now stands." 2. "If ye town obtains a vote to remove ye bell and belfry, to see if ye town won't think it proper to pass a vote that the persons that removed it from ye place where ye town last voted it should at their own charge remove it to ye place where ye town shall order it." 3. Upon a request of a number of the inhabitants, "to see if the town will pass a vote for ye bell to stand for ye future upon ye town's land where it now stands." 4. "For ye town to do what they think proper relating to ye bell and belfry." The town "Voted to 'sett ye bell and belfry' at some convenient place at ye East end of ye school house." The belfry was accordingly placed where the town voted, and it stood there as represented in the Doolittle picture on the 19th of April. Subsequently, a door was cut in one side, and the town hearse was kept in it.

The Third Meeting-house of Lexington, erected by the Town in 1794, as seen from Monument Street, near the Residence of the late Hon. Charles Hudson, and looking toward Main Street. The Tower of the Baptist Church seen in the distance. It was destroyed by Fire in 1846.—*From Barber's Historical Collections.*

When the new meeting-house was built in 1794, it was sold to John Parker, the father of Theodore Parker, and carried away to the Parker homestead, where it long did duty as a wheelwright shop and where it is still standing. Soon, we trust, under the auspices of Lexington Historical Society, it will come creeping back, to find its final resting-place near the spot of its birth. It should be placed on some height overlooking the village, and restored to its original form, a bell procured of the exact size of Deacon Isaac Stone's gift, the old tongue put in it, and on every anniversary of the 19th of April it should be rung, to let people know how the summons sounded which called the minute-men to the Common on that eventful morning.

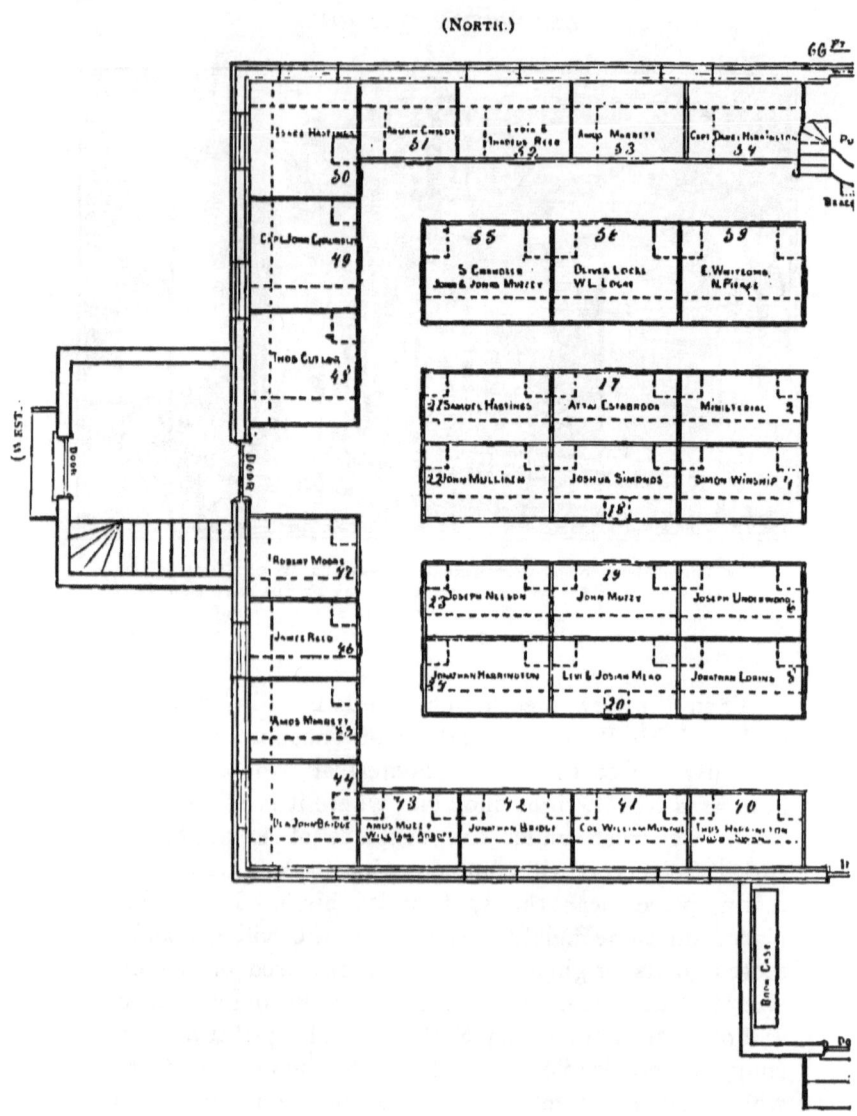

The Interior of the Third
[For List of Pew

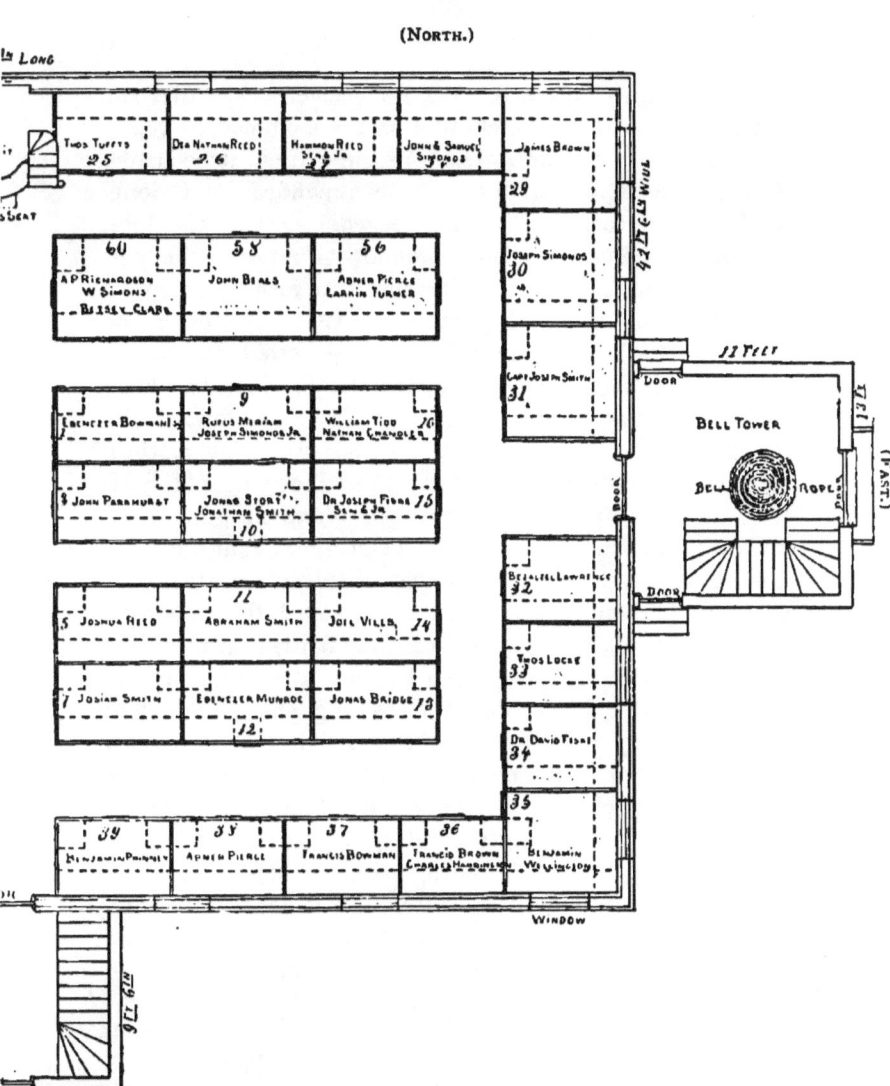

Meeting-House of Lexington.
Owners, see Appendix.]

On the 19th of April, 1822, forty-seven years after the battle, the event was celebrated on the Common by representing it as nearly as possible in the manner it occurred. A company of minute-men was commanded by Colonel William Munroe, the orderly sergeant of Captain John Parker's original company. About twenty of the survivors of the battle were present, and formed again on the very spot where they stood on that day, under the direction of the same man. The line rested upon Bedford Street, near the point where the bowlder has been placed, and extended across the Common, toward the monument. The men were in their work-day clothes, like the minute-men of 1775. They bore the old flintlock muskets, many of them the identical guns used on that day; and Jonathan Harrington, the original fifer, gave them the shrill notes of his old instrument. Colonel Benjamin Wellington commanded the red-coats, personating Major Pitcairn of the British army. He rode a spirited charger, which became almost unmanageable under the firing; but the rearing and plunging of his steed were regarded by the spectators as a part of the acting, admirably done. The red-coats marched in on the double quick, and formed just behind the meeting-house, Colonel Wellington riding a little in advance. Then, in imitation of Pitcairn, using probably the same words, more forcible than polite, he commanded the minute-men to disperse; but they stood their ground, and, drawing his pistol, he fired and commanded his men to fire. This was followed by a second volley, that brought to the ground a number of our men. Then came the rush of the red-coats, with fixed bayonets, upon Parker's little company, and the command for them to retreat. In like manner, Colonel Munroe personated Captain Parker, using his strong language, now inscribed upon the bowlder, and adding, "Them is the very words Captain Parker spoke." It was arranged that two men should run from the meeting-house, where they had gone for powder, and that at a certain spot one should fall by a British bullet, as in the original scene. And so it was acted; but the criticism was made that he recovered too soon after being killed, and took his place among the living. Thus the battle was fought over again on the Common, before hundreds of spectators, without bloodshed; and minute-men and redcoats remained good friends after it was over, treating each other liberally at the taverns.

One of the pleasant reminiscences associated with Lexington Common, by some of our elderly people, relates to the visit of General Lafayette in 1824. On the morning of Thursday, September 2, he was received by a troop of horse and a cavalcade of citizens at the line of West Cambridge, where a salute was fired by the Lexington Artillery Company. From this point he was escorted up Main Street to the Common, where an arch had been erected, trimmed with evergreen and flowers, and bearing the inscription, "Welcome, friend of America, to the birthplace of American Liberty." Here another salute was fired; and, standing in front of the monument, an address of welcome was made by Elias Phinney, Esq , to which Lafayette feelingly responded. He was then introduced to fourteen survivors of the battle, taking the hand of each as they passed by. All the school children of the town were present, the girls dressed in white, and the boys in their best Sunday clothes, each wearing a badge with a picture of Lafayette printed on it, and bearing a bouquet. As they marched by, they threw their flowers at his feet. A great multitude gathered on the Common and along the streets, waving handkerchiefs and shouting, "Welcome, Lafayette!" It was a scene of wild and joyous enthusiasm, — the homage of the people to their country's noble friend and benefactor. A parting salute was given him, and, escorted by the military companies and half the population of the town to the line of Lincoln, he rode on to Concord, where a similar reception awaited him. A lady now residing here, then a child too young to attend the reception, remembers that she was rewarded by her father and mother with a sugar image of Lafayette, on their return, which was long and reverently cherished as a memento of his visit.

But perhaps the most noteworthy occasion connected with the history of Lexington Common, excepting the 19th of April, 1775, was the removal of the remains of those who fell in the battle from the old burying-ground to a stone vault prepared for them in the rear of the monument. This occurred in 1835, on the sixtieth anniversary. The 19th of April coming that year on Sunday, the services were held on the following day. The remains were taken from the common grave, where the bodies were originally interred, placed in a box lined with lead and enclosed in a mahogany sarcophagus, upon which were carved eight urns, representing the number of the slain. This was borne from the cemetery to the meeting-house, followed by ten survivors of the battle, and escorted by the military companies of the town and a long procession of invited guests and citizens of Lexington. The sarcophagus was deposited in the broad aisle in front of the pulpit, where a platform had been built for the orator of the day. A great congregation had gathered to witness the ceremonies, crowding every part of the house and filling the staging erected outside on a level with the windows. It was an inspiring audience, including many of the most prominent and distinguished men of the State, among whom were Chief Justice Story, President Quincy of Harvard College, Daniel Webster, and Lieutenant Governor Armstrong. The oration was given by Edward Everett, then in the zenith of his fame; and it is safe to say that no more eloquent, stirring, and finished production ever fell from his lips. Though occupying two hours in its delivery, he held the attention of the people to the close, often kindling high enthusiasm by his marvellous power. At its conclusion, the procession was reformed, and, marching around the Common to the monument, deposited the sarcophagus in its final resting-place, while the military companies fired three volleys over the sacred spot. It was a scene of solemn and touching interest. Several of those who witnessed it had seen the bodies of the slain brought from the Common where they fell into the meeting-house, and there laid upon the floor. They had seen them placed in boxes made of rough boards, and borne away to a common grave amid the lamentations of their kindred, neighbors, and friends, full of anxious forebodings concerning the issue of that direful event.

And now, after sixty years, they saw the grave reopened, and the mouldering relics reverently gathered up and placed in a new tomb, near the spot where the heroes fell; while the people of the town and State proudly honored their memory. Truly, it was an impressive scene, and one long to be remembered in Lexington.

But I pass on to briefly notice the building of the third meeting-house, which was determined upon at a town-meeting held March 11, 1793, by a unanimous vote. A proposition of Governor Hancock to give $100 toward it whenever the town began the work, and of Rev. Jonas Clark to add $30 more, probably hastened this action. But, when the question of the location and place of the new house came to be discussed, this unanimity quickly disappeared; and it required seven town-meetings, occupying nearly a year, to settle these important matters. After an attempt to place it at the geographical centre of the town, wherever that might be, and after voting to have it face down the Great road, and to build the tower on the end towards the Concord road, it was finally agreed as a compromise that it should face half-way between south and south-east, that the tower for the bell should be set on the easterly end, that the house should stand twenty feet farther back into the Common, and have three porches with stairs to the gallery from each. Accordingly, it was so built. It had a central aisle, an aisle along the four sides, and two aisles running from east to west, with fifty-eight large square pews on the floor and twenty-four in the gallery, besides seats in the gallery for the negroes. The cost of its erection we do not know; but it was more than defrayed by the sale of the pews, all of which were disposed of at auction on the 23d of December, 1794, the highest bringing $174. The town chose Isaac Hastings vendue-master, with John Mulliken for his clerk, and directed that the price should be in dollars, and no bid less than half a dollar should be received. When a pew was put up, a flag was to be hoisted over it, and inscribed "*for sail.*" No means of warming the meeting-house were provided at first; but, subsequently, two enormous stoves were put in, with pipes running around the entire building. This addition to the people's comfort, however, was stoutly opposed by a considerable minority; and one man was so offended at the innovation that he never attended meeting afterward.

It was voted to paint the exterior "a pea green"; but the interior was not painted, and no man was allowed to paint his pew "without a consent from the town." The dedication of the new meeting-house took place on the 15th of January, 1795, at 11 A.M., under the direction of Captain John Mulliken, Captain John Chandler, and Samuel Downing, the committee chosen by the town; and the day was given up to the imposing ceremonies and to great social festivity and rejoicing. This edifice remained substantially as it was built until 1846, when, after extensive and costly repairs, on the night before it was to be rededicated it took fire and was burned to the ground. The society did not rebuild on the Common, but located on Elm Avenue, fronting it on the north side. Thus the old site ceased to be occupied for a church, after having been used more than a hundred and fifty years.

There is no mention of an enclosing fence to the Common before 1820. Up to that time it lay open, and roads and paths ran across it in various directions. But in November of that year the town voted to build a fence around the Common, of oak posts, with two bars or joists between, to cost $1.50 per rod; and it was built accordingly. Dr. Stillman Spaulding, Daniel Chandler, and Samuel Downing were the committee to carry out the vote of the town. After the completion of the work, it was moved in town-meeting that the fence should be painted; but the proposition was voted down as a piece of extravagance, not to be tolerated. Two years afterward, however, the proposition to paint the fence, at an expense of $30, was carried. The fencing of the Common was not done originally for the purpose of putting it in better condition and beautifying it, but for the income to be derived from renting it as a cow pasture; and the committee having it in charge were instructed to ascertain before building it the probable annual rental, which they reported to be $15. The sum actually received, I believe, was $12, which was generously devoted to the education of the children in the schools. Shrewd, careful men ruled Lexington in those days, from whom we might well learn lessons of practical economy in these extravagant days. This fence of oak posts and rails stood for twenty years. In January, 1840, the town voted to build a new one in its place, of split stone posts and joists, at a cost not exceeding $350, besides the materials in the old one. Here, again, appears the careful, saving spirit of the people of Lexington half a century ago. The money was to be taken from the town's portion of the surplus revenue, and the rents of the Common to be applied to reimburse the fund to the amount so used. Nothing is done for this precious spot made forever sacred by the blood of the martyrs of freedom; nothing is done for it because identified with the town's history from the beginning, and with that event which has given Lexington honor and glory throughout our country; nothing is done for it on account of the greater attractiveness and beauty which it might give to the village: but it is fenced in that it may be made available for a cow pasture, and the income used to pay the cost of enclosing it!

Let us be thankful that a nobler spirit rules in Lexington to-day. The years which have gone have brought some appreciation of the glory that forever encircles Lexington Common. The town has just expended nearly $2,000 in its improvement, making it as beautiful as it is sacred. What the fathers regarded only as so much common earth the sons and daughters regard as holy ground. Let it be kept clean and bright in the years to come, that the thousands who visit it from far and near may see we are not unworthy possessors and guardians of the birthplace of American Liberty!

ROBERT MUNROE.

READ BY G. W. SAMPSON, OCT. 12, 1887.

AMONG old Lexington families, the Munroes stand second to none. In civil life or in time of war, they were always found at or near the front. Perhaps the three most distinguished in the Revolutionary period were Robert, Edmund, and William. I am here to speak for Robert, not because he was superior in any way to the others, but because he was my ancestor. Robert Munroe was born in Lexington, May 4, 1712.

The old stock of Munroes first settled, as I am told, in that part of Lexington which takes its name, "Scotland," from their nationality. They can be traced as far back as the time of Bruce in Scotland. We read of them at Bannockburn, Berwick, Edinburgh, in the Protestant war in Germany, in Sweden, and even in India, fighting sturdily and steadily on every occasion. Up to 1651 the Munroes could boast of three generals, eight colonels, five lieutenant-colonels, eleven majors, more than thirty captains, and a large number of subalterns. We find the Munroes again in command of large forces in the Irish Rebellion, at Fontenoy, at Falkirk and elsewhere; everywhere, indeed, but in the rear, when there was fighting at the front.

It is an old saying that "blood will tell." When a military spirit becomes infused through generations, it only needs a spark of war to ignite the latent energy in a man and develop a first-class soldier. It follows with almost as much certainty as if he were a chemical compound, the occasion for the display of warlike attributes being the missing link in the component parts. We read with no feeling of surprise, therefore, the name of Robert Munroe as ensign of the Lexington quota in the French and Indian War. In the expedition against Louisburg, in 1758, he was color-bearer in that memorable attack, reflecting honor upon Massachusetts and upon Lexington. In 1762, he was one of a company from this town sent to watch the Indians, and prevent the reopening of hostilities before peace had been declared.

In regard to his private life and characteristics, I can give no information. Those who knew him at all, passed away more than a generation before my time; and those who knew him intimately, more than two generations. He seems to have been a typical New Englander of that period, firm, upright, of staunch integrity, but of considerable bigotry, superstition, and prejudice; a grand old Puritan, who abhorred idleness, dishonesty, and all things superficial, who constantly attended church, trained in the militia, kept a sharp eye on public affairs, tilled his farm, and cheered his sorrow with good New England rum, after the custom of that time.

He had four children: Anna, wife of Daniel Harrington; Ruth, wife of William Tidd; and Ebenezer and John. Daniel Harrington, my ancestor, was clerk of Captain Parker's Company at the time of the battle; and William Tidd was lieutenant. Both were afterwards prominent in town affairs, and lived to a ripe old age. From some of the elder members of my family I have heard many anecdotes of "Grandfather Harrington" and his blacksmith shop, and of "Uncle Bill Tidd," as they were familiarly called. Ebenezer and John Munroe, like most of the young men of the town, were in the events of the 19th of April, Ebenezer also seeing service in the Jersey campaign of 1776.

April 19, 1775, was the last day on earth of Robert Munroe. When aroused from his bed by the message of Paul Revere, it would have been pardonable in a man of sixty-four, who had twice seen service, to have acted on the principle of "old men for counsel and young men for war." He might well have decided that his family was fully represented on the field by his two sons and sons-in-law. But it requires a more vivid imagination than I possess, to think of Robert Munroe as hesitating for one instant.

In the band of minute-men, Munroe and his family played an important part. Lieutenant Tidd was next in rank to Captain Parker; Daniel Harrington was clerk of the Company; Munroe himself was ensign, and next in rank to lieutenant; while his two sons were privates. Thus the father and his sons and sons-in-law all stood in line on the Common. At the first volley, the old hero was struck down. Much as I dislike a man who holds himself aloof from his fellow-men on account of the superiority of his forefathers, I believe that a proper feeling of pride in one's ancestry is fitting and right. When I think of that brave old man, and scores like him, I say Lexington people have as good blood in their ancestry as any people of the Commonwealth.

"What the fathers won the sons defended." I was reminded of this sentiment last Memorial Day, when the grave of one of our soldiers was being decorated. Over the spot where he rested stood the color-bearer and Commander of the Post, all three — the living and the dead — direct descendants of Robert Munroe.

Two other descendants of his enlisted from a neighboring city during the Rebellion, and there were probably others who followed their example. Some have predicted that this country will degenerate through a lack of interest in her welfare; but I believe that we shall always have men in time of need of the spirit of Robert Munroe, who will spring to the front, and bravely defend what the fathers won.

CAPTAIN JOHN PARKER.

READ BEFORE THE LEXINGTON HISTORICAL SOCIETY, DEC. 14, 1886, BY MISS ELIZABETH S. PARKER.

THE earliest mention in history of the name of Parker appears about the eleventh century. He was a Norman, a follower of William the Conqueror, and was a keeper of the royal parks, hence the name, which we find variously spelled. The branch of this scattered family to which we trace our ancestry more directly sprang from a family of Browsholme, Yorkshire, which came to this country from Lancashire. It seems to have been of some note in the sixteenth century. The Parker coat-of-arms was emblazoned with a leopard's head, stars, and a stag pierced with an arrow, for a crest, with the motto, "Semper aude." But we care very little to trace mottoes, coats-of-arms, or even English aristocracy in a family that claims a John and a Theodore Parker.

Fifteen years after the landing of the Pilgrims, Thomas Parker, born in 1607, sailed from London, and settled in Lynn in 1635, and was made freeman two years later. He was probably driven to this country on account of his love of religious liberty, as the Parkers appear quite frequently among those opposed to the Established Church of England. He was one of the seven founders of the First Church in Reading, to which place he removed in 1640. Thomas's grandson, John, came to Lexington, then Cambridge Farms, in 1712, one year before the town was incorporated. The homestead which he purchased in the south part of the town has been in the family ever since, a period of one hundred and seventy-five years. We next come to Josiah, the father of our subject, John, who died in 1760. All of these in regular succession, Thomas, Hananiah, John, and Josiah, we learn from the records, were men prominent in both town and church. They were selectmen, town-clerks, assessors, and two of them lieutenants. They were members of the church, and held high places in the "seating of the meeting-house."

Had I, when a child of eight or ten years, possessed the wisdom or the desire which I now have, I could give many incidents of our great day in Lexington and many characteristics of my great-grandfather. My grandfather, Robert Parker, Captain John Parker's youngest son, died when I was too young to have any remembrance of him. But my grandmother was also of Revolutionary ancestry, the daughter of Joshua Simonds, who on the day of the battle, being separated from the company, was in the gallery of the meeting-house where the town's powder was kept, and, placing the muzzle of his gun in an open cask, determined to blow up the building, should the British enter. She used often to try to entice me from play, to listen to the tale that was of burning interest to her. But her wishes were seldom heeded, and it has been a life-long regret to me that the golden opportunity was lost. Thus my paper to-night is robbed of what might have been a great charm.

Captain John Parker was born in 1729, and passed most of his life in the daily toil of the farm, with few pleasures and many hardships. He was a stout, large-framed man, of medium height, somewhat like his illustrious grandson, Theodore Parker, in personal appearance, but had a much longer face. He was fond of reading, as we learn from Parson Clark's diary that he was one of those who often borrowed the minister's books, regarded as great treasures at that time.

In 1755, he married Lydia Moore, whose parents lived, if I have been correctly informed, not far west of the present town farm, in a house which many years since was in ruins.

I think no sketch of Captain Parker should be written without noting the influence which Parson Jonas Clark exerted upon him, and upon the church and town, and even upon the whole State. The old meeting-house on the common was not only the storehouse of the powder of the minute-men, but it often rang with the stirring words of that patriot priest, urging them to make good use of that powder. Mr. Clark's youngest son, Harry Clark, whom I knew very well, often visited at our home, and spoke of the intimacy and friendship of the Clark and Parker families. Captain Parker would probably have had no name in history, had not the events and circumstances of the time led the British to Lexington. The whole of Middlesex County was equally awake to the momentous issue. It needed only a spark to kindle the fire of liberty, and any village green might have been the scene of the first encounter. But are such events accidents? Are not man's chances God's opportunities? Was not sturdy Miles Standish the fitting captain of the Plymouth Colony? Was it an accident that Abraham Lincoln was President of the United States at the time of the nation's awful peril?

The result shows that Parker was the man fitted for the

occasion. Not bravery alone was required, but cool judgment as well. He had served in the French and Indian War; and, although he was much younger and had seen less service than many of his company, he was chosen by those patriots to command, and proved a worthy leader of a noble band. In his company were a brother and two cousins. Of one of the cousins, Everett says, "History does not furnish an example of bravery that outshines that of Jonas Parker"; and Bancroft writes: "A wound brought him on his knees. Having discharged his gun, he was preparing to load it again, when as sound a heart as ever throbbed for freedom was stilled by a bayonet." Captain Parker, on the evening of the 18th, when rumors of the anticipated march of the British reached him, hastily left his home and family. He had a wife and seven children,— four girls and three boys, the eldest boy only fourteen and the youngest four. He knew not what to expect. Perhaps he was about to die, as some of his company did, even on their own door-steps.

It is a cool, moonlight night. With many doubts and fears, the early hours are passed. At two in the morning, by the ringing of the bell from the old belfry and the beating of the drums, the men are called from their firesides, but are soon dismissed. At half-past four, as

> "Slowly the mist o'er the meadow is creeping,
> Bright on the dewy buds glistens the sun,
> When from his couch, while his children were sleeping,
> Rose the bold rebel, and shoulders his gun."

Parker calls the roll of his company. Then comes the command, "Every man of you who is equipped follow me, and those who are not go into the meeting-house, and furnish yourselves from the magazine, and immediately join the company." Then the line is formed near the meeting-house.

After this comes the order to load the guns. One of the number speaks, "There are so few of us, it would be folly to stand here." Captain Parker sternly replies, "The first man who offers to run shall be shot down." The British approach, and Pitcairn cries out, "Disperse, ye rebels!" but they firmly stand their ground, and Parker says, "Don't fire unless fired upon; but, if they want a war, let it begin here." But not till the regulars have fired and many have fallen does the order come to disperse. All this has occupied but a few minutes, but the die is cast. War has begun.

The British pass on to Concord, having killed or wounded one-quarter of the brave band. Captain Parker again gathers his company, and follows the British to Lincoln. As they are seen returning, he leads his men aside into an open field; and they fire once more upon the enemy. Early in May, Captain Parker led a part of his company — forty-five men — to Cambridge upon call of the Provincial Congress, where they served from the sixth to the tenth of the month. Again, on the day of the battle of Bunker Hill, he is at Cambridge, with sixty-one men ready for action.

During this time, his health had been feeble; and the exertions of the day and the excitement of the time produced such an effect on his nervous temperament that he died of consumption a few months afterward, Sept. 17, 1775, only forty-six years of age.

He who was so brave and true at the beginning of the struggle saw not the end nor the glory.

I think we can say of Captain John Parker that he was

a man of no little mental and executive ability, of strong will, bold, earnest, and daring; a man sure of his convictions and true to his convictions. Jonathan Harrington, the last survivor of the battle, said that on that day "he looked as though he could face anything"; and most bravely did he face the responsibilities of that trying time.

There hang in the senate chamber of the State House in Boston two priceless relics of Captain John Parker,— one the fowling-piece which he carried on the 19th of April, 1775, and the other the first gun captured from the British in the War for Independence, both gifts of Theodore Parker to the State. May they ever be regarded with reverence, and

"Tell to our sons how their fathers have died"!

Although many years have passed away since our forefathers gathered on the common to resist the invaders, the grave of Captain John Parker has never been marked until recently by a memorial stone. In 1884, the town appropriated the sum of $1,500 to mark spots of historic interest in Lexington; and, among others, the grave where his remains were supposed to rest received a substantial and fitting monument, bearing this inscription: —

TO THE MEMORY OF CAPT. JOHN PARKER,
COMMANDER OF THE MINUTE MEN, APRIL 19TH, 1775,
BORN JULY 13TH, 1729, DIED SEPTEMBER 17TH, 1775,
THE TOWN ERECTS THIS MEMORIAL,
1884.

A FEW WORDS FOR OUR GRANDMOTHERS OF 1775.

READ BY MISS ELIZABETH W. HARRINGTON, DEC. 14, 1887.

THE number of those who have had personal communication with the witnesses of the opening events of the War of Independence is now very small; but fortune favors me in having an uncle and aunt still living, Mr. and Mrs. Otis Munroe, of Boston, respectively eighty-eight and eighty-six years old, both with clear minds and good memories, from whom I have gathered a few facts told them by eye-witnesses, which may be of some interest to others.

Looking back a hundred years and more, I find that my numerous great-great-grand-parents, uncles, aunts, and cousins, composed a large portion of the scant population of Lexington at that time. You must pardon me, therefore, if I talk much of my family. From Ensign Robert Munroe, my great-great-grand-father, prominent in the military events of our history previous to the 19th of April 1775, and who was the first man to give his life to save us from British oppression, down to those of us who joined the great army of women, and from 1861 to 1865 were found in the hospitals or in our homes, scraping lint, rolling bandages, sewing woollen shirts, and knitting woollen stockings for our brave men, each generation has furnished those who have served their country well.

In a house standing between those of George Harrington and Mr. Gould, back of the Common, lived my great-grand-parents, Daniel and Anna (Munroe) Harrington, with seven or eight children. His blacksmith shop stood next to Jonathan Harrington's, the house in which Mr. Gould now lives. There must have been little sleep in those houses on the night of the 18th, when danger was abroad, and the roll-call of Captain Parker's Company was heard at two o'clock in the morning. About seventy minute-men gathered on the Common; but they were dismissed, and recalled at four o'clock, when the British troops were actually approaching. Probably no word of farewell was spoken by Daniel, as he, with his son Levi, hurriedly left his wife to take his place in the company. His son, my grandfather, then but fifteen years old, was drummer; and both were present when Robert Munroe fell. Think of the agony of Mrs. Harrington when, in the dim light of dawn, the dreadful firing began in front of her own house, and she soon learned that her father was killed, while her husband and son were standing before the volleys of the British. She doubtless saw her neighbor, Jonathan Harrington, reel with outstretched arms toward his wife, who had also witnessed the terrible scene from her window; but he dropped dead before she could reach him. Those women had never seen the horrors of war; and it must have seemed to them that an avalanche of British soldiers had fallen upon our village, and all their defenders were to be killed before their eyes. After seven men were killed and nine wounded in the short space of twenty or twenty-five minutes, the troops moved on to Concord, and quiet was restored,— the dreadful quiet in contrast with the heavy tramp of soldiery and the startling and unusual sound of firearms, the quiet of death.

Let us look in upon those two houses back of the Common, each with a brave man lying there, who half an hour before had sprung from his bed to seize his musket and rush to death. Those poor women could not tell what the next hour might bring forth. How could they let their precious dead remain in their homes when at any moment the British might return, ready to finish the diabolical work of the morning? They had no time to indulge their grief: they could scarcely realize what had happened. They had no time even to pay proper attention to the wounded, but must hurry away to a place of safety. The sparse neighborhood afforded few sympathizing friends to offer help and condolence. Quite likely, each was alone in her home, or alone with young children, and each filled with anxious thoughts for the safety of others dear to her.

And what must have been the distress of others, who in a place of safety heard the sound of guns, when every shot might be carrying death to those whom they loved! All sorts of vague rumors reached them. It was reported that the slaves were about to rise, and murder the defenceless women and children. How their hearts must have quailed, when the danger long threatened now seemed so near! Without the excitement of being under arms which animated the men, they had only the thought of the danger and perhaps death of their fathers, husbands, and sons.

Tuesday, the 18th of April, 1775, must have been a day of great apprehension. On the spot where the Russell House now stands picture to yourself a low, unpainted house, in which lived my great-grand-parents, Matthew Mead and his wife, with their daughter Rhoda, then about eighteen years old, and two sons, sixteen and fourteen. While the men of the families were on the alert for news, the women were looking after the comfort of their households. On that day Rhoda and her mother had filled the great brick oven with the beans and brown bread so dear to the Yankees of that day as well as this. Early in the evening a sound of horses' feet rapidly approaching their door must have given their excited nerves a shock. As Rhoda looked out, she saw three mounted British officers draw rein at the house,—probably three of the ten sergeants sent out by General Gage, who dined at Cambridge and then scattered along the different roads out of Boston, to prevent any knowledge of the expedition reaching the country. As the wind blew aside their cloaks, so bright was the moon that she distinctly saw their red coats. Imagine the terror of Rhoda and her mother as these men entered without ceremony, and insolently helped themselves to the day's baking, taking the steaming brown bread and savory baked beans from the oven. If Rhoda's cheek paled with terror when she saw these men enter, can you not picture her indignation bringing back the color, as she stood there in her homespun gown, homeknit stockings, and stout leather shoes, watching their bold impudence? If they left Boston early in the morning, though they did dine at Cambridge, their cold, windy ride made the bread and beans, hot from the oven, a savory dish for them. We are not told of any conversation between them and the ladies whose kitchen they were raiding; but we can imagine what it might have been.

When Rhoda's father and brothers came in for their supper, the father having spent the day in anxious conference with his neighbors, oiling and repairing their muskets and pistols and sharpening their swords for possible need, how their blood must have boiled as they heard who had been there, and saw the empty table! Little supper or sleep for the father that night, spent as it must have been in preparing to take his family to a place of safety, which he did early in the morning of the 19th. The women and children were carried to Mr. Reed's, in Burlington. When John Hancock was persuaded to retire to the same place, brave Dorothy Quincy, to whom he was betrothed, accompanied him.

Wednesday, the 19th, was a day of far greater trial to the women than Tuesday, the 18th. Nearly on the spot where the house stands built by the elder Mr. Sherburne lived another of my great-grandmothers, Lydia Mulliken. Think of her trials on that day when the British were returning from Concord. She was the widow of Nathaniel Mulliken, the famous clock-maker, whose name may be seen on many of the tall clocks treasured by lovers of antique furniture. His shop was quite near his house. Mr. Hudson, in his History of Lexington, does not mention his occupation; but he was the grandfather of Mrs. Otis Munroe, and she remembers the fact. Whether by his clock-making or by some other means, at his death, eight years before, he left his widow a large property Early in the morning of the 19th, as the dreadful news flew along the road of the approach of the British, there was a hurried hiding and burying of Mrs. Mulliken's silver and other valuables. The silver was hidden in the well near the shop, probably the one which is still there. My aunt now owns one of the spoons hidden in the well. It has Lydia Mulliken's initials on it. My grandmother, Rebecca Mulliken, then a girl of thirteen, often spoke of her great regret that she had not hidden with the silver a pocket which with great pride she had embroidered with crewels, but which was lost in the fire. On the return of the British from Concord in the afternoon, they burned the house and shop, and she lost above four hundred and thirty pounds.

The people of Menotomy, now Arlington, suffered greatly, and especially the women. One woman, Mrs. Adams, lying ill in bed, with five children hidden under it, had the shock of seeing the bed-curtains drawn by a soldier who pointed a bayonet at her breast. But he allowed her to escape. She threw a blanket around herself and her babe, and crawled away to the corn-barn. Everything in the house was taken, including the communion service of the church, which was kept there, and the machinery out of a tall clock, the case of which still remains an heirloom in the family. The buildings were then fired; but the flames were soon extinguished, and they were saved. In fact, few houses escaped after the retreating British had rested themselves under the protection of Lord Percy. Think of the return of Mrs. Jason Russell of Menotomy to her home from a place of safety, to find there, lying side by side in their own blood, her husband and eleven others! Many instances are remembered of the bravery of the women of those trying times. The letters of Mrs. Abigail Adams to her husband, while he was in Congress at Philadelphia, should be read by all women and men, in order to realize at what cost our fore fathers and mothers gained our blessed independence.

MATTHEW BRIDGE.

READ BY HARRY W. DAVIS, FEB. 8, 1887.

THE Bridge family has been identified with the history of Lexington from its earliest settlement. They have shown themselves to be an energetic, upright, religious family, and interested in everything that pertains to the welfare of the community.

There were two Bridges, John and Joseph, in Captain Parker's Company, on the Common, on the 19th of April, 1775; and in the Revolutionary War we find in the records that there was a Bridge in various expeditions and battles. At Bunker Hill and White Plains, and wherever work was to be done or battles fought, a Bridge was ready to do his share; and, when in 1861 the "sons were called on to defend what the fathers had won," the Bridges did not shrink from the trust bequeathed to them, but, shouldering their muskets, helped to preserve the Union.

John Bridge, the earliest ancestor of the family in America, was born about the year 1578, during the reign of Queen Elizabeth, in Braintree, Essex County, England. He came to the New World in 1631 or 1632, with what was called the Hooker Company, which settled in that part of the Massachusetts Colony then known as New Towne.

In 1634, Hooker, thinking the settlement was becoming too crowded, obtained from the Great and General Court leave for enlargement or removal. He accordingly removed to Connecticut with the larger part of his company. But John Bridge made up his mind to stick to his new home; and by his efforts Rev. Thomas Shepard came from England to become the pastor of the few who remained after the withdrawal of Hooker.

To John Bridge, therefore, are ascribed indirectly the founding of the present city of Cambridge and the establishment of Harvard College, since by his efforts Shepard came to the New World, and by Shepard's efforts Cambridge was founded and Harvard College established. John Bridge appears to have been a man of good common sense, upright, conscientious, and religious. He held honors in the town of Cambridge, being on the first Board of Selectmen, first deacon of the church, and a member of the General Court.

Matthew, the subject of this sketch, was the son of Matthew and Anne (Danforth) Bridge and the grandson of John. He was born in Cambridge, in the year 1650, on a spot which has become historic. The Bridge homestead was on what is known as the Craigie estate, where Washington had his head-quarters while in Cambridge, and recently the residence of Longfellow.

Matthew seems to have inherited the traits of his father and grandfather, being of a sturdy spirit and of strict integrity. He came to Lexington, then Cambridge Farms, some time between 1660 and 1670, his father having owned land here as early as 1643.

In 1682, James Cutler, Matthew Bridge, Jr., David Fiske, Sen., Samuel Stone, Sen., Francis Whitmore, John Tidd, Ephraim Winship, and John Winter petitioned the General Court to be set off as a separate parish; but the petition, being vigorously opposed by the people of Cambridge, was not granted, and, though renewed at various times, it was not until 1691 that a committee reported favorably, and the parish was established the next year. We find that Matthew Bridge subscribed £1 toward the building of the first meeting-house, after the organization of the parish.

He was married in 1687 to Abigal, daughter of Joseph and Mary Russel, from which marriage there were nine children. He served as a soldier in King Philip's War, and also in the ill-fated Canadian expedition of 1690. He was also chosen on town and precinct committees, and filled at some time nearly every office, his first being that of constable in 1693. He was on the committee to "treat with Nibour Muzzey about ye purchas of a parcell of land lying northward of ye meeting-hous." This is now Lexington Common, and no one subscribed a larger sum toward the purchase.

On the death of his father in 1700, being the only surviving son, he inherited a large tract of land situated south-westerly of Vine Brook, and comprising about six hundred acres.

Upon the incorporation of the town in 1712, he was elected selectman, town clerk, and town treasurer, and was re-elected to the same offices in 1713, showing that he possessed the esteem and confidence of his townsmen. He served as "clerk" of the parish prior to the incorporation of the town, being first chosen in 1698, and continuously until 1714. He was treasurer of the town from its incorporation in 1712 until 1716, inclusive. At the town-meeting March 5, 1716, it was voted "that Mr. Matthew Bridge, Treasurer of said Town, should have three pounds allowed him for the first two years he kept the Town Treasury and twenty shillings a year afterward annually to whoever sustaineth that office." It is a curious fact in regard to the salary of the town treasurer that this sum of one pound remained the salary for several years, without any endeavor to increase it. In 1732, Matthew Bridge, Jr., being treasurer, he had the following article inserted in the warrant: "To see if the Town will gratifie Mr. Matthew Bridge, Jr., his request for more allowance than what was usual, for his services as Treasurer." This certainly showed a progressive spirit in the Bridge family, but let us see how the request was treated.

In the records of the May meeting in 1732, we find the following: "Voted to see if the Town would grant the Treasurer, Matthew Bridge, Jr., more than his usual allowance for that service, and it passed in the negative."

Again, in 1747, there appears in the warrant, "By a request of Mr. John Bridge, Town Treasurer, to see if the town will allow him two pounds old tenor per year for serving the Town as Treasurer"; and the following action was taken on it: "Voted one pound old tenor a year to Mr. John Bridge for serving the Town as Treasurer."

It seems strange that the sons of the first town treasurer should have been the only men filling that office who remonstrated at the paltry allowance. Matthew Bridge was one of the committee to provide the first schoolmaster "that will answer the law." Captain Joseph Estabrook was appointed.

On the seating of the second meeting-house, according to the vote passed, " The vacant room from the easterly end of the pulpit by the wall of said house to the easterly door, is granted to five persons, first next the pulpit to

Mr. Matthew Bridge seven foots and one inch," etc. This was doubtless considered an honorable position, and he was awarded it both on account of his age and his extensive lands.

He was admitted to the church in 1718. Upon the marriage of his four sons, he built each of them a substantial farm-house, and presented each with one hundred acres of land. These houses are still standing, and in a good state of preservation. The house built for his son Matthew is situated in Waltham, beyond the present residence of Mr. Cornelius Wellington. John occupied the house where Messrs. Estabrook and Blodgett now live; Joseph, the house where Nehemiah Wellington lived, now owned by Mr. O'Brien; and Samuel, who was my ancestor, the house owned by Mr. Tompkins.

Matthew Bridge died in 1738, at the advanced age of eighty-eight years. He lived an upright and honorable life, and was respected and honored by his townsmen. Many descendants of the Puritan, John Bridge, have become distinguished, and will always be identified with the history of our country,— a President of the United States, a cabinet officer, generals, and others, but I doubt if there has been or will be one of stricter integrity or more upright character than Matthew Bridge.

Long may the affairs of Lexington be directed by as able and conscientious men!

REMINISCENCES OF A PARTICIPANT IN THE OCCURRENCES OF APRIL 19, 1775.

READ APRIL 12, 1887, BY GEORGE O. SMITH.

Mr. President,— I desire to offer for the acceptance of the Society the spectacles worn by Mrs. Mary Sanderson, together with her pocket-knife, and the mortar and pestle which were a portion of her marriage outfit.

The knife was presented to me by her grand-daughters a few days after the decease of Mrs. Sanderson, and has been in my possession since. The mortar has been mine by promise for some time, but, being in use by the family, has only come into my possession within a few days. It has been used by three generations,— the youngest of the third being more than sixty years of age,— and in common use one hundred and fourteen years. The spectacles I received a short time since from her surviving grandchildren for the purpose of presentation to the Society, if deemed acceptable.

Many of our older residents will remember Mrs. Sanderson as "Old Lady Sanderson," or "Grandma Sanderson," names by which she was familiarly known.

Born in this town before the dawn of the Revolutionary period, a wife and mother at the time, and an eye-witness of the opening scene of the conflict, in which her husband took part, she was the last remaining of those venerated worthies, save Jonathan Harrington, and a connecting link between those memorable times and our own.

A few reminiscences incident to her long life and residence in this town may not be inappropriate at this time.

Mary Munroe, a daughter of William Munroe, Jr., and Rebeckah Locke, a great-grand-daughter of William Munroe, Sen., who came to this country in 1652, was born Oct. 10, 1748, in the north-easterly part of Lexington, then called "Scotland" because of the number of Scottish settlers residing there, the location, it has been said, being selected because of its resemblance to the scenery of their native country.

This section I have always understood to be the district lying east and north of the residence of Mr. George Munroe, extending to the vicinity of the residence of the late Mr. Hugh Graham on the north and to the town line of Woburn on the east.

On the 22d of October, 1772, when twenty-four years of age, she married Samuel Sanderson of Waltham, a carpenter, or, as the old lady in later years termed it, "a jiner"; and they went to live in the house now standing, and occupied by Mr. Ellery I. Garfield, next south-east of the old "Munroe Tavern," her husband using the basement for a workshop. Of Mr. Sanderson little is known, aside from the fact that he was a member of Captain Parker's company, and took part in the events of April 19. He was an unassuming and rigidly pious man. In those days, the carpenter or joiner was the coffin-maker; and Mrs. Sanderson related that many a night she had held the candle while her husband stained the "narrow house" of some departed neighbor or townsman. In this house they resided on the 19th of April, 1775.

On that morning, on the alarm being sounded and assurance given that the British were *really coming*, Mr. Sanderson gathered his little family, consisting of his wife Mary, their infant child, and a little girl who lived with them; and, taking such articles as they could hurriedly collect and carry in their arms, by the light of a lantern he piloted their way to a refuge,— the home of her father in the new Scotland.

Coming within sight of lights in her father's house, he left his treasures in safety, and, hurriedly returning to his home, made all as safe as possible against the depredations of the enemy, and repaired to the rendezvous of Captain Parker's company.

Mrs. Sanderson, on arriving at the house of her father, found her mother preparing breakfast for her two sons, one of whom, disbelieving the story of the advancing soldiery, was loath to rise and take so early a breakfast.

After the British had retreated to Boston, on returning to his home, Mr. Sanderson found his house sacked, many articles destroyed, and their cow, a part of Mrs. Sanderson's marriage portion or dower, killed, and a wounded British soldier quartered upon them.

Toward evening, Mr. Sanderson went for his wife; and, on learning of the depredations of the British soldiers, she was greatly exasperated, declaring she would not return to harbor and take care of the British soldier. She asked her husband why he did not "knock him in the head," saying she "would not have him in the house," and that she "would do nothing for him,— he might starve."

But the town authorities said he must be taken care of, and he remained. The soldier begged for tea; but she insisted he should have none, saying: "What shoold I gie him tea for? He shall hae nane." And she gave him none till her father told her, if she had any, to give it to him, and he would make it up to her from his own stock.

Mrs. Sanderson, being of Scottish descent, and living among Scotch people in her youth, gave a Scottish accent to many words. "Should" and "would" she pronounced "shoold" and "woold," and "have" and "give" as "hae" and "gie."

Her earlier feelings of hatred for her country's enemies continued in her old age, and I remember well her excited manner and indignant tones whenever she spoke of them or of their doings. "The *Satanish* critters," she said, "stole and destroyed everything in the house, and didn't leave rags enough to dress the wounds of their own man." When over one hundred years of age, Mrs. Sanderson described with minuteness many articles of her wardrobe and household goods which were destroyed or missing, rarely failing to mention the cow, and that she was a part of her marriage portion.

So plainly was Mrs. Sanderson's dislike of the wounded man shown that he refused food or drink till first tasted by some of the family, evidently fearing he might be poisoned. This may be accounted for by the old lady's reply when asked, "Well, grandma, what *did* you give him?" "Oh, I gae him all he wanted, and every now and then I gae him a *diivilish honing*."

Many incidents were related by Mrs. Sanderson connected with the early history and struggle of the colonies for freedom, which, had they been recorded, would be of priceless value now.

In my boyhood, I saw her almost daily, and had a fondness for questioning her of the happenings of the Revolutionary days; and, could I remember the answers she made to my boyish questions, a much more interesting account of her might be given. She lived to see the fourth generation, herself making the fifth, and could say, in fact, "Arise, daughter, go to thy daughter, for thy daughter's daughter hath a daughter," a great-great-granddaughter having been born to her.

In 1776, with her husband she moved to Lancaster, where she resided until his death in 1800, when she went to live with her son Samuel, in Waltham, residing with him till his death in 1829. Subsequently, she lived with a grand-daughter in Weston; and in 1837 she returned to reside with the widow of her son Samuel in East Lexington.

A distant relative of Mrs. Sanderson, writing of her a short time previous to her death, says, " She returned to reside with her old friend, the widow of her son Samuel, with which incomparable woman and her two daughters she has resided for the last fifteen years."

When Kossuth visited Lexington in 1852, the escorting cavalcade halted, and Kossuth paid his respects to her. Meanwhile, the band played " Yankee Doodle," the favorite air of the old lady, greatly to her delight.

Mrs. Sanderson was of a lively, cheerful temperament, and quick and facetious in reply.

When past one hundred years, a distant relative — a young clergyman — complimented her upon her fair complexion and former personal attractions. "Ay," she replied; "and it was lucky for you, young man, that you were not about in those days."

As I remember her, though always in a sitting posture, because of her inability to stand or walk, she seemed of tall and slender physique, with a pleasing expression of countenance. In her age, she was not unattractive; and one would judge might, in her younger days, have been possessor of more than ordinary personal attractions.

Said a relative: "She was one of the most slender of her family, and hence, perhaps, her uncommon care of herself, seldom, if ever, going abroad after sunset. To this care of herself, her plain, simple manner of living, and the salubrious air of her native town, may be attributed her great longevity." "Until above seventy, when her power to move about began to fail her, she continued to be an active, industrious woman, fulfilling the duties of wife and mother while her husband lived, and giving valuable aid for many years in the home of her son — a farmer — and in the nurture of her grand-daughters, who, in her years of age, faithfully repaid her care of them."

When past ninety, she could use her needle, and sewed upon many useful articles for her friends.

Her Bible and "Watts's Hymns," together with the "Farmer's Almanac," were her constant companions. The "Farmer's Almanac" was daily consulted by herself or her attendant for her benefit.

On account of her extreme age and participation in the events of the Revolution, it was a custom of clergymen exchanging with the pastors in the village to call upon "Grandma Sanderson"; and her grand-daughter told me that, on one occasion, being told that the minister was below and coming up to see her, she quickly took her almanac and slipped it under the rug at her feet, saying, "I woold na read sich a book on the Lord's Day, but I woold na give him cause to think I might."

Her sight returned to her when past one hundred, and she read aloud without glasses.

Something more than a year before her decease, she became a helpless paralytic and a constant care. Even then she understood what was said to her, and noticed what was taking place about her, but was unable to express herself with distinctness, though understood by her relatives, and in the last hour of her life inquired the condition of the weather. Her death occurred on the 15th of October, 1852, at the age of one hundred and four years and five days.

It would be interesting for one competent to do so to trace the great historic events and changes and to note the advance in material progress during the compass of this single life. To fully comprehend and realize them would seem impossible.

The French and Indian War, the War of the Revolution, of 1812 with Great Britain, and the Mexican War were all begun and ended during her life.

The "Stamp Act," the duty on tea and imports, the "Boston Port Bill," and all those parliamentary and aggressive acts which led to a separation of the colonies from Great Britain, were enacted after she was nearly seventeen years of age; and it is probable an independent existence for the colonies had not been dreamed of by the most sanguine patriot till after she had arrived at womanhood.

From the narrow limits occupied by the thirteen colonies, sparsely populated, and without unity of government, had grown a union of thirty-one States, extending from ocean to ocean and from the lakes to the Gulf of Mexico, with a population of twenty-five millions.

The steam-engine and electric telegraph, perhaps the

two most important inventions in their influence upon civilization, and the cotton-gin, one of the most important inventions in its effect upon American commercial progress, were brought to light, and their use and benefits adopted or realized by every civilized nation of the world, during her lifetime.

These, in a degree, help to realize her extreme age; and I need not trespass further on your time or patience.

The surviving grandchildren of Mrs. Sanderson are: Mr. Chester Sanderson, now of Brookline (who is eighty years of age); Mrs. Caroline Goodnow and Miss Elizabeth H. Sanderson, of Waltham, to whom we are indebted for this tender of the spectacles worn by their venerable ancestor.

AMOS LOCKE.

READ BY HERBERT G. LOCKE, DEC. 14, 1887.

It is not strange that the descendants of those brave men who stood on Lexington Green on the 19th of April, 1775, in defence of the rights of America, should seek to honor their names.

Amos Locke, of whose life and characteristics I propose to give a brief outline, was great-grandfather of the writer. His name is found enrolled in Captain Parker's famous company of minute-men. He was born in Lexington, Dec. 24, 1742, two and a half miles from the centre of the village in a northerly direction, on the farm owned by his father. The house stood where the house occupied by his grandson, William Locke, now stands, on the pathway known in those days as "Dog Lane," and which would possibly be known in these progressive days as "Dog Lane Place."

The house in which he was born was taken down about 1830. The estate has been owned by his descendants to the present time. Amos and Reuben Locke, cousins, grandsons of Joseph Locke, Sen., both resided in the old house. Joseph Locke was a descendant in the second generation of Deacon William Locke, one of the first settlers of Lexington, who was born in Stepney Parish, London, Dec. 13, 1628, and came to this country when he was but six years of age in the ship "Planter."

I have been unable to obtain the maiden name of Amos

Locke's mother. Her given name was Sarah. The family were remarkable for their longevity, his father dying at the age of eighty-six years and his grand-parents at the advanced age of ninety years. Amos Locke, when a young man, received the education common to young men of those days, and when not engaged in his studies labored on the farm. He was married to Sarah Locke in 1769. She was an orphan, adopted and brought up by Thomas Locke. Amos Locke found in her a diligent coworker and partner in his struggles, receiving words of encouragement when the way looked darkest, and cheerful companionship when resting from his daily toil. She survived her husband by seven years, dying in July, 1835, at the age of eighty-four. They had four children, all of whom were sons.

In 1776, June 14, his father sold to him, for the nominal sum of twelve pounds, his part of the house and portions of several pieces of land in Lexington and Woburn. On the same day, he gave his father and mother a lease of the same premises during their natural lives, and engaged to provide them with good nursing in sickness and under the infirmities of advanced age until their death. He became a large owner of real estate, having bought, in addition to the home farm, all the land now belonging to Mr. Phelps's farm on Adams Street. William Locke, uncle of the writer, holds a number of old deeds and documents, one of which, I think, is signed by the king. Amos was not what would be called a rich man, but simply well-to-do, intelligent for the time, an industrious tiller of the soil, earning his bread by the sweat of his brow, and performing his part in an honest and respectable manner. When the alarm came on that memorable morning, he was up, and ready to perform his duty faithfully and earnestly. The alarm spread rapidly through Lexington at two o'clock in the morning; and he hastened to the scene of action, coming across lots over the hill by George Wright's house and by Warren Duren's to the common. On his arrival, a messenger, who had been sent towards Boston, returned, and reported that he could not learn that the regulars were coming. This threw some doubt upon the correctness of the alarm of Paul Revere. The weather being cool, the company was dismissed, some returning to their homes, and others going to the Buckman Tavern. He started towards home, but had not proceeded far when he heard the sound of the drum summoning him back. I know of no better account of the part he played in the subsequent events than that given in the following affidavit. It reads as follows:—

I, Amos Lock of Lexington, in the County of Middlesex, testify and declare that between two and three o'clock on the morning of April the 19th, 1775, I heard the bell ring which I considered as an alarm in consequence of a report that John Hancock and Samuel Adams were at the house of the Rev. Jonas Clarke, and that it was expected that the British would attempt to take them Therefore Ebenezer Locke and myself both being armed, repaired, with all possible speed, to the meeting-house; on our arrival, we found the militia were collecting; but shortly after, some person came up the road with the report, that there were not any regulars between Boston and Lexington, consequently we concluded to return to our families. We had not proceeded far, before we heard a firing, upon which we immediately returned, coming up towards the easterly side of the common, where under the cover of a wall, about twenty rods distant from the common, where the British then were, we found Asahel Porter of Woburn shot through the body; upon which Ebenezer

Lock took him, and discharged his gun at the Britons who were then but about twenty rods from us. We then fell back a short distance, and the enemy soon after commenced their march for Concord.

AMOS LOCK.

MIDDLESEX, SS.   Dec. 29, 1824.

Then the above named Amos Lock personally appeared, and made oath to the truth of the foregoing affidavit by him subscribed, before me.   NATHAN CHANDLER,

Justice of the Peace.

I have been unable to gather much information of his doings from 1776 until about 1810. At that time he was employed in a grist-mill as tender. The mill was located at Thomas Locke's pond on the Middlesex turnpike. The pond is familiarly known at the present time as "Granger's Pond." When business was dull at the mill, he would return to his farm, which was but a short distance from the mill; and, when farmers came to have their corn ground, they would take from the beam a large horn and blow it, and he would hasten to answer their wants, the horn being kept there for that purpose. I believe later he became owner of this mill. The writer's Uncle William says he has seen him in winter put on his snow-shoes and take a bushel and a half of corn on his back, jump over the wall, and start off to mill to grind it, and bring back the meal to make bread for breakfast. The snow-shoes are still in existence. It was a favorite pastime of his to amuse his grandchildren by narrating some of his hunting expeditions, while they were gathered about a blazing fire of four-foot sticks. They would seat themselves on a bench extending into the side of the fireplace, while he sat exactly in front of the fire; and the whole scene would be brilliantly illuminated by a small pitch-pine stump, laid on the blade of an old hoe and made fast to one side, forming a most striking picture. Thus he would sit for hours at a time, and entertain those gathered about him. I will endeavor to tell one of his stories, which seems so fabulous as hardly to be credible, but is nevertheless true. He said that, during one of his exploits with his old flint-lock gun, he killed at one shot just as many pigeons as there are weeks in the year, fifty-two. The pigeons in those days used to fly over in large flocks. He would build a booth, or hut, in which to conceal himself. On the outside of his hut he would have what was known as a "sweep," or, as we should say, a well-sweep. To the end of this he would attach a live pigeon, and then shake the sweep: this pigeon would flap its wings as the flock approached, and attract their attention, when they would come down and cover the sweep and the ground. And on one occasion he shot, as I have stated, fifty-two, or, as he expressed it, "just as many as there are weeks in the year, at one shot."

Amos Locke was not without his peculiarities. He always cut his food with a jack-knife and ate it from a wooden plate. He used to point out with pride a landmark that divided his farm, the shin-bone of a horse, which remained in the rear of the house for a long period. The dividing line in front of the premises ran through the centre of the old well.

In disposition he was of an even temperament, loving his neighbor as himself, and doing unto others as he would like to be done by. It is said of him that he never spoke ill of his neighbors or fellow-men. He believed in doing all he had to do well. After a long, lingering illness, he was called from earth on the 27th of July, 1828, dying in the house where he had always lived, at the age of eighty-five years.

Thus ended the life of one of those brave men who was willing to seal the cause of American liberty with his blood. Surely, the descendants of those patriots should glory in the heritage of freedom which the fathers bequeathed.

THE OLD TAVERNS OF LEXINGTON.

READ BY EDWARD P. BLISS, DEC. 13, 1887.

It is probable that few towns in New England suffered a greater change than befell Lexington in consequence of the construction of railroads. The Lowell Railroad was built in 1835, and the Fitchburg in 1842; and each decade since has compassed more transformations and new ways of living than were wrought in each half-century before. I have been to many of the old people and asked them to talk of Lexington as it was before railroads diverted travel and the transportation of goods from the old cart-roads. I have awakened their memories of the ox-loads and the four, six, even eight, horse loads of the products of the once profitable farms of New Hampshire and Vermont,— great wagons laden with grain or piled with wooden ware or packed with homespun woollens and many other commodities,— on the way to the markets of Boston, or returning from the seaport with groceries, cotton goods, salt fish, and the many other necessities and luxuries that commerce brings from over the seas. Old villagers recall the stage-coaches and the names of the drivers. Seventy-five years ago Lexington was busy with coming and going. The roads were sometimes blocked with teams, and often at noon-time forty wagons would be drawn up before a tavern or the stores. The twelve taverns were none too many, and their accommodations were pressed to a degree unendurable to our habits. Two beds in a room and two lodgers in a bed was the rule. Twelve taverns! Where were they? Six of them are still standing hospitably close to the roadway.

The most antique, and now nearly two centuries old, is the Buckman, built by Benjamin Muzzey, who owned the land, and in 1693 was licensed to keep public house; and it is supposed that from the first a sign hung before it promising entertainment for man and beast. It was painted a yellow-white, and the roof was green. The dormer windows were built in when it was a century old. The low ell running out cornerwise is as old as the house, and is framed into it. In it was the first store, and in 1812 the first post-office in Lexington. The tavern sign hung from a post a little distance south-west of the house. There were formerly six out-buildings. The largest stable stood north of the house, partly where the sidewalk now runs; and the road was then about two rods nearer the common than at present. The ash-trees on the road were set out by John Buckman more than a century ago, and were then on his land.

To all who become used to the proportions of this house there comes a conviction that the carpenters were also intelligent architects. The roofs were expanded so as to brood over house and home. The honest timbers are frankly displayed in the dining-room, and the fireplace in this room is arched over with picturesque effect; but this construction was for the purpose of accommodating the floors above. The studding of the rooms on the lower floor to the right of the entry is lower than on the other side, while the chambers above are reversely higher and lower. There were nine open fireplaces, one of them set in brown Dutch tiles. The double chamber on the north side of the second floor, and the four chambers in the roof, were for guests.

On the *Nineteenth of April*, 1775, we find that John Buckman was the landlord. He was then thirty years old, a member of Captain Parker's Company, and in his public house the patriots assembled the night before the battle. When the company drew up on the Common some of their number, or perhaps sympathizing fellow-patriots, must have remained in the tavern; for shots were fired at the British from the tavern, and a volley returned, the bullet-marks of which are still visible. Miss Mary Merriam, now ninety years old, relates that she has often heard her father, who was then a boy of thirteen, say that he stood on the steps of the tavern that morning, and that some men — as she expresses it — "who wouldn't stand up for their country" were near him, and they said that the British would not fire on them, as they were brothers; but, when that volley was fired at the house, they scrambled to the attic and cellar, — the boy with those in the attic.

On the retreat of the British, two wounded soldiers were brought into the house, one of whom died there and was buried with others in an unmarked grave in the old burying-ground. John Buckman died in 1792. Of his personality we know little, but he was a jovial man and fond of a joke. One evening an old toper brought with him a few pennies to buy rum to take home; the landlord, remarking that he supposed the old fellow would rather have his rum than anything else in the world, was answered that nothing could induce him to give up the bottle he was taking off. The toper started away with his rum It was a dark night, and he lived back on the

Concord road. John Buckman snatched a candlestick that had a contrivance that snapped like the click of a pistol, and followed the man to the lonesomest spot, and then, suddenly clicking the candlestick, put the cold metal to the neck of the terrified man, demanded everything he had with him, and got the rum. That was a fine story to tell for a few days; but shortly after Buckman was arrested, and fined fifty dollars for highway robbery, and afterward he kept his peace.

Joshua Simonds came into possession of the tavern on the death of Buckman, and in 1794 sold it to Rufus Merriam, his son-in-law, on condition that he should keep a public house. Before consenting he brought his children to sleep there for a night, to try if they could endure the noise. He had the date 1794 painted on the sign. A stage-coach stopped at his house; and his business was rather in providing meals than in furnishing lodgings. His custom was more with "carriage-folk" than with teamsters. Balls and parties were given here. One especially notable occasion was when a fashionable company from Boston engaged the house and grounds for a day, to celebrate the close of the War of 1812, and erected a marquee, or tent, for dancing. The ladies were served a fine dinner by themselves in the double chamber, and the gentlemen had to find for themselves in neighboring taverns. There was a guard stationed about the grounds to exclude Lexington people. This house was seldom opened as a public house after 1815.

The sister tavern to the Buckman was the Munroe, built in 1695. We cannot think long of these two old houses without calling up in imagination the sleepers in the old burying-ground. Under these roofs and around these chimneys gathered those who had left pleasant country places in old England to make new homes in "Cambridge Farms," as Lexington was then called. What an omission never to be remedied, it is, that these people did not bring with them the English habit of calling their homes, or clusters of houses, or the hills and woods, by names significant and imaginative! And why did none of them take pains to pass down to us some Indian names? These two old houses, let us hope, will stand till some Scott or Hawthorne shall people them with picturesque ghosts, and reopen the mysterious wine-cellar under the Buckman, now for so long time solidly walled up.

The Munroe Tavern was built by William Munroe in 1695; and the next year he was licensed to keep a house of public entertainment. The front half of the house is the oldest part. John Comey, William's brother-in-law, succeeded him as landlord. In 1770, William Munroe, a descendant of the first owner, bought the house of Buckman, added the rear part, and reopened it as a public house. Afterward he built an ell on the north side, the gable end of which was toward the road. The upper room of this ell was a dance-hall on occasions; but there were usually in it several beds. The lower room was a shop or store. The Hiram Lodge of Free Masons was organized in the hall, which they long used as a lodge-room. A few years ago this ell was removed.

The Munroe Tavern was occupied on the day of the battle by Earl Percy, who rested here to collect his re-enforcements. The house was sacked by the soldiers, and an inoffensive old man was killed while trying to escape from the rear. Several of the wounded soldiers were brought in, and their wounds were dressed. We are glad it was the good fortune and great honor of that landlord and patriot, William Munroe, to entertain as a guest in his house President Washington, who came to Lexington in November, 1789, and dined in the double room of the second floor on the south-east side. The boys climbed into the elm-tree, still standing before the front of the house, to get a sight at Washington.

Jonas Munroe succeeded his father William as landlord; and he experienced the highest prosperity of tavern-keeping days until the railroads turned away the course of travellers. The Munroe Tavern was always a home-like and inviting place. The doors were never locked. Many parties, or balls, as they were ambitiously styled, were given here. The two landlords, William and his son Jonas, were specially endowed with the qualities of heart and manner which make up a host under whose care it is a blessing to fall, This public house was rather a public home to townspeople and to strangers. On the sign was a punch-bowl.

Lydia Tidd, widow of Daniel, was licensed to keep a public house in 1699. Her husband died in 1696, leaving her the care of two children. Perhaps her prosperous father-in-law, then an old man, let her have the use of the old Tidd House in North Lexington, which was his property; or we can imagine that she independently set up for herself and her children in some other house which long ago lost its reputation as a tavern.

The next in age of the Lexington taverns was that which stood on the old Concord road, about two miles from the Buckman. It faced the old road, now little used, and was invaded by the British soldiers and the bar ransacked. It was called the Bull Tavern, and Daniel Childs first kept it. In 1820, Joel Viles bought it; and it continued a tavern until after 1850. It was a large house, had long barns on one side for horses, and space in sheds on the other side for forty yoke of oxen, so much were those creatures then made of service. The sign was a bull: hence it was called "Bull Tavern."

A little tavern which I have included in the twelve is the Hoar Tavern, which is just within the precincts of Lincoln. Some of the American patriots, meeting to harass the British on their retreat, had lunch in this house. It was first kept by John Hoar, then by Leonard Hoar, and lastly by Joseph L. Hoar. It was not altogether a public house; but it was a place at which a meal or a bed could be had. Mr. Sherman lives there now.

Most affectionately remembered by our old men is the Dudley Tavern, which stood north of the brick house opposite the flagstaff on the Common. Nathan Dudley came to Lexington in 1790, and soon after opened this tavern, which he kept till 1835. It has been entirely removed. It was very popular with teamsters, who stopped here for dinner only; for it had small accommodations for lodgers.

Mr. Dudley made such good flip, and was so happy to have his neighbors come in, that it is said, after great snow-storms, before the roads were broken open, footpaths would be shovelled from all directions in the neighborhood up to the Dudley Tavern, and the rigors of winter forgotten in good fellowship and a mug of flip. On Sundays, between services, the women and children would eat their lunch in Mr. Dudley's parlor, and the men would collect in the bar-room and purchase gingerbread and cheese. Mr. William Locke, now eighty-five years old, can remember once being in that bar-room after morning services; and old men were seated in a semicircle before a peat fire, passing a great mug of flip from one to the other, and talking over the French and Indian War, in which some of them had taken part. A hundred and fifty years back in oral history can one bright old man take us, who still lives in this town!

The largest and most considerable in the busiest tavern-keeping times was the Monument House, built in the year 1802, by Amos Muzzey, three years after the monument was placed on the Common, for which it was named. It stood on the site of the present Town Hall. It had a gambrel roof, with two dormer windows, and was painted yellow. It was first kept by Amos Muzzey, afterward by John Parker, —— Haywood, Oliver Locke, Samuel Chandler, Elias Mead, and last by J. D. How. In 1847, Mr. Benjamin Muzzey, who owned the property, tore down the old house and built a hotel costing over $20,000, which passed through several hands, and was burned down in 1867, having been occupied lastly by Dr. Dio Lewis for a girls' boarding-school.

This old Monument House was the most prosperous of all the taverns, and is the oftenest spoken of by old travellers. The sign about five feet square, with edges cut in ornamental curves, hung thirty feet high on a post over the pump and trough. The devices on the sign were emblematical of good cheer. On one side was a white-frocked butcher, standing by his cart, on the side of which was painted a sirloin of beef. On the reverse side of the sign were two fat oxen, red and white, one looking over the other's back.

Many public dinners and balls were given in this house;

and sleighing parties came here on winter nights. In a frame in the Massachusetts House there are cards of invitation to these entertainments. The oldest reads : —

This card admits bearer Mr. Nathan Chandler to the Ball at Mr. Muzzey's Hall, Lexington, on the first of January, 1811. To commence at 5 P.M.

Thos. Johnson, Samuel Mulliken, Oliver Locke,
Managers.

Sometimes the dancing commenced at four o'clock; and the custom was to dance till the same hour in the morning,— twelve hours of brisk dancing to a single fiddle, with a lunch of cream toast! There were two open fireplaces in this old dance-hall.

It is related that a half-crazy fellow named Chaplin, always acting under the illusion that he was a great soldier, and sometimes even an entire army, one day came into the Monument House, where he was familiarly known, and assuringly said to the landlord that he thought he had sense enough to have a glass of grog. After some banter, the landlord gave him a drink, which he swallowed with gusto, and then calmly remarked that he guessed he hadn't cents enough to pay for it, and went out, leaving the landlord to take the guys of his other guests with the best grace he could.

Up in North Lexington there is a neighborhood of well-built white houses. Across the road from the two-centuries-old cottage is the Simonds Tavern, built with brick ends. It has two large chimneys and two front doors, between which was the bar-room, doubly easy of access. There were two kitchens ; and there must have been good business here, for it was enlarged at the southern end. There was a large room which could be used as a dance-hall, in which was a double row of beds. In the parlor at the northern end the antiquarian will enjoy the panelling, the heavy cornice, and especially the chimney mantel-shelf, high and narrow, and under it a generous fireplace, framed in blue and white Dutch tiles with Bible pictures. This tavern was kept by Joshua Simonds from 1802 till 1828.

The second house beyond this was also a tavern. John P. Reed lives in the house now. It was built by Christopher Reed in 1822. The parlor is the only room that remains as it used to be. The room at the left of the hall was the bar-room; and the bar itself was in a little room now removed. There was the usual large convertible dance-hall bed-chamber in the ell, now moved back, which formerly stood in line with the front of the house; and the large barn, now turned about, stood then lengthwise in line with the rest of the establishment.

The Davis Tavern stood where the Catholic church now is. From 1833 to 1843 it was kept by Joseph Davis, who came here from Princeton.

A house just beyond the boundary in Burlington was the Richardson Tavern, standing at the junction of the Burlington road and the Lowell turnpike. Three stages stopped here, and two of them changed horses, thus bringing to the dining-room and the bar much custom. The ceilings of the rooms in this house are almost oppressively low. There was once a dancing party given here, attended by some Lexington young people, one of whom, now quite old, remembers that a great, strapping fellow, prominent in the dancing, suddenly interrupted the gaiety by falling in a pretended faint; and, with prompt appliance of resources nearest at hand, they brought him to by pouring down his throat a bowl of oysters.

THE OLD TAVERNS. 83

On the Concord turnpike, a few rods from the Theodore Parker birthplace, stands a large house with brick ends, kept by William Simonds as a tavern from 1810 till 1828. Why so many fine old buildings were constructed with brick ends I have failed to learn.

This tavern often accommodated forty lodgers; but it was one of the earliest of the taverns to fail of custom, and it was kept rather as a road-house than a place for lodgers. In those days, when prosperous farmers of New England parentage lived in the south part of the town, there was a dancing-school in this tavern, and many parties were given here.

In East Lexington there was the Old Bowman Tavern, which at first consisted of two houses joined together, the older of which was taken down in 1843. The landlords were Bowman, Brown, Spear, Wyman, then Lemuel Lakin, for whom it was called "Lakin's Tavern." He kept it from 1833 till 1840, and was succeeded by Flint, Fields, and the last landlord, James W. Colburn. It has been a private dwelling-house since 1843, and is now occupied by Henry Webber. This tavern had a good share of custom. In the busy season forty horses were put up.

Another tavern stood where the Willard House now is, and was kept by Stephen Robbins; and afterward it became known as "Cutler's."

The management and the customs of these public houses, and the thrifty yet kindly ways of the landlords, with their hearty, boisterous, ever-changing households,—these are the topics it is fascinating to set the old men talking about. The tavern-keepers were mostly farmers, and always large buyers of the produce of neighbors.

Hay and grain sold at good prices, and were largely raised here. There were no servants, but "helpers,"—all American born and equals. The wives superintended the kitchens, and were the cooks. Their own or neighbors' daughters waited at table. On fine occasions there were two black women who came in to serve, dressed all in white. They were named "the Tulips." Boys worked in the stables; and man's as well as woman's work was never done.

The landlord, besides being everywhere and knowing everybody, usually dispensed the beverages at the bar; for toddy, black-strap, flip, and hard cider were drunk by nearly all, from ministers to teamsters. Although there was much liquor used, drunkenness was not common; yet the bad effects of alcohol were in various ways apparent. It is instructive to consider how free the use of rum was in those times, by men of English and Scotch descent, and to see how it was not legislation, but good sense, that brought them to abstain from it. Our ancestors, newly come from Europe, used intoxicants as freely as the newly arrived Irish do to-day. Is it not reasonable to expect that climate, example, and good sense will have the same effect on them, making them naturally and not perforce abstainers?

In old times, New England rum was the common drink, sold at wholesale at twelve and a half cents a gallon, and at three or five cents a glass. Flip — not made anywhere now — is remembered fondly by old folks,— a most "insinuating" drink one of them calls it. It was made of home-brewed beer, sugar, and a toss of Jamaica rum, stirred in a mug with a red-hot iron,— called a "loggerhead,"— which made it boil and foam, and gave it a burnt, bitter flavor. When a company were seated before the fire, one great mug of it was passed around,— the loving cup. So common a drink was it in winter-time that the loggerhead was always kept in the fire.

The charge for a lodging in half a bed was ten cents, afterward twelve and a half cents. Breakfast and supper were each twelve and a half cents. Dinner was twenty-five cents. Horses were put up for fifty cents, which seems high; but they were well fed, and grain was costly. We can see why the farmers dreaded the railroads, and abused them as bringing ruin to the country, just as some provincials speak now of commerce.

Some saving teamsters brought fodder for their horses and a box of food for themselves, paying only ten cents for a lodging, and, of course, something for grog. Yet they were welcome to the taverns, as swelling the current of business; and gridirons were hung about the bar-room fireplace for their free use.

Breakfast was served at about half-past four o'clock in summer and at five in winter, as the teamsters must get on the road early. It was a good meal of beefsteak, mutton chops, eggs, and often roast chicken, as poultry-keeping had a large share in tavern economy. Pie was often served at breakfast. Dinner was a real country repast, usually something boiled, though the tin kitchens could produce never-again-to-be-equalled roasts. We can imagine the drivers, with vigorous appetite, tearing the meat with two-tined forks, and passing it to the mouth on broad-bladed knives.

Before we serve supper, let us see who are the arrivals in town during the day. Mostly, they are the drivers of loads of merchandise from the back country, some even from Canada, meeting others just out from Boston. There is loud interchange of news and the gibes of good fellowship. Let it be a November afternoon. There are forty wagons in some of the barns. There have come into the town droves of cattle, sheep, and hogs, which are yarded near by. Unfortunate men were the two who arrived just before sundown, one going ahead in a cart and dropping corn and the other afoot in the rear of a straggling, erratic procession of a thousand turkeys. Their misfortune lay in not getting over Concord hill before sundown; for, as soon as it began to darken, the fowls, gobbling, halting, stopped and craned their heads toward the trees along the road, and no urging would move them onward. One and another, and then all the rest, flew up into the branches, and soon were quiet, except for the breaking of a limb and a moment's disturbance. Those turkey-drivers would have been much happier, had their turkeys roosted all over the Munroe Tavern and the out-buildings, and themselves secured the hospitality of Uncle Jonas. The drivers of a flock of geese two days before had arrived in good season. But, when the turkeys were in the trees, and the dusk deepened into darkness, the men rode rapidly into town, mindful that they must anticipate the sunrise in awakening their charge, and calling them into line by scattering corn. But they missed great sport at the tavern; for a little earlier "Priest" Muzzey swaggered up, loud-voiced and rough. He had been an itinerant minister, but was now a tavern loafer. Uncle Jonas was feeling somewhat Herculean himself that afternoon, and, after a moment's banter, he threatened to lay Priest Muzzey on the cold earth. There was a rush together, a struggle, and —

Uncle Jonas was the under half of that heap of struggling humanity. No one could more cheerfully endure to be laughed at than that amiable man; and every onlooker among his guests felt that, if there were still a charm in his making flip, the vanquished would be the triumphant host before bedtime. Let us yield to the kind welcoming of that ideal tavern-keeper, and be present ourselves before the big fireplace in the dull glow of the peat embers, and get the tidings of the day, talk politics, and have our hearts as well as ideas enlarged by face to face discussion.

And now, having brought the day to its close, and realizing that we live in a new age, can we not distinctly recognize that the hospitable spirit of those old tavern-keeping days prevails still? for have not many of us felt that the sentiment of Lexington to-day is,—

"*Come in and make yourself at home*"?

LEXINGTON ACADEMY.

READ BY A. E. SCOTT, APRIL 12, 1887.

THE Lexington Academy and its building have been identified with the history of Lexington to such an extent that a short paper regarding them seems desirable.

I find by the county records that the land between the Clark House, on Hancock Street (which was the old Bedford road), and the Common was part of the estate of Rev. Jonas Clark.

In 1819, the heirs of Jonas Clark, the deed being signed by Thomas Clark and fifteen others, conveyed to John Augustus, described as a cordwainer, who lived in the house now occupied by Mr. James Gould, between eight and nine acres of land, bounded by the town's Common, the old and new roads leading to Bedford, and other land of the estate, the consideration being $1,100.

Mr. Augustus conveyed to the Trustees of Lexington Academy a part of the same land, described "as being near the meeting-house and containing about half an acre," and as "beginning on the south-easterly corner by the old road leading to Burlington, and by the town's Common, thence running northerly by said road nine rods to a stake and stones, thence running westerly about twelve rods to a stake and stones at the new road leading to Bedford, thence running southerly by said road nine rods and ten feet to the town's Common, thence running easterly by said Common to the bounds first mentioned."

"For the purpose of erecting an Academy by the name of Lexington Academy and for such other purposes as the said trustees and their successors shall think best to promote the designs of the institution."

It appears that the people of Lexington were thus early interested in better educational advantages than the town schools afforded, and resolved to establish an Academy not only for their own pupils, but also for all who might be drawn here from other towns.

Great interest was felt in the project, and nearly all of the leading people subscribed liberally.

From the records in the office of the Secretary of State, I find that, by an Act of the Legislature in 1822, a charter was granted, establishing "an Academy by the name of the Lexington Academy," "for the purpose of promoting religion and morality, and for the education of youth in such of the liberal arts and sciences as the trustees for the time being shall direct," with power to hold property, the income of which should not exceed three thousand dollars.

Rufus Meriam, Esq., Dr. Joseph Fiske, John P. Meriam, Esq., Dr. Stillman Spaulding, Nathan Reed, John Augustus, Joshua Simonds, Joseph Simonds, Christopher Reed, Nathaniel Harrington, William Chandler, Aaron P. Richardson, Thomas Tufts, Nathaniel Harrington, Jr., Nathan Dudley, Hammond Reed, Ebenezer Simonds, Thomas Greenleaf, Jonathan Munroe, Francis Wyman, and William Smith, Jr., were appointed Trustees.

They appear to have proceeded at once to purchase the land and to erect the building which is now occupied by the Hancock Congregational Society. The building seems to have been well constructed, and to have been superior to most school buildings at that time. It contained a fine hall in the upper story, which, with other conveniences, was furnished with a large fireplace at each end, affording ventilation and good cheer, and which added brilliancy to many occasions, not the least of which was the grand ball that closed the exercises of dedication.

Rev. Caleb Stetson was the first principal, assisted by John Wright. By the first catalogue of the institution,— July, 1823,— it appears that the school was started under very favorable auspices. Eighty-four students from several States were enrolled, seventeen being from Lexington. Those from other towns lived with different families in the village. Mr. Stetson remained in charge of the Academy three years, and was followed by Mr. Wright, Mr. Sherman, Mr. Huntington, Mr. Hager, and Mr. Russell; but its early years seem to have been its most prosperous ones. It had no endowment from which an income could be received, it failed to continue self-supporting, and was finally given up. The early graduates seem to have felt an affectionate regard for the institution. They formed an association called the Lexington Academy Association, which held reunions in Lexington for many years after the Academy was discontinued.

Other teachers, Mr. Houghton, Mr. Whitney, and Mr. Blodgett, and Mrs. Trask, leased the building at different times; but their schools were not long prosperous, and it was finally closed.

In 1833, the Trustees of the Academy sold the property, with "one cast-iron stove and pipe," to Austin Chittenden. This is the last record I have been able to find of the doings of the Academy. What was done with the funds received from the sale of the property, or how the affairs of the Corporation were settled, does not appear.

In 1835, Mr. Chittenden sold the property, with the same stove and pipe, to Timothy P. Ropes. It appears from a catalogue in my possession that Mr. Ropes and Samuel Stetson established a school, which they called "Lexington Manual Labor Seminary." The object of the school, as the prospectus states, was "to blend useful instruction and innocent recreation with habits of industry and profitable labor; to furnish youth with agreeable exercise; to make them acquainted with the use of mechanical tools and with mechanical operations, also with horticultural pursuits." Thus one of the earliest experiments in industrial education was tried at Lexington.

For the purpose of carrying this plan into effect, the prospectus says, "We have taken the commodious academical building in this village, together with a mechanical shop and sufficient land for our purpose." The scholars were allowed to employ their leisure hours in the shop or garden; and the products of their labor were to be received at a fair price toward their tuition.

The basement of the Academy was fitted up for the shop; and the land around the building, and probably a larger lot near by, were used for the planting of trees and a garden. The window-blinds on the house formerly of Captain Phelps are said to have been made there, and at times there were sales of articles made in the shop; but I have not been able to learn many details.

The triangular piece of land now in front of the Hancock Church was cut off from the town's Common by the laying out of the new Bedford road, and Mr. Ropes asked the privilege of setting trees upon it; but objection was made in town-meeting that, if allowed, it might be doubtful whether the trees would be the property of the town or of Mr. Ropes.

The plan of the school seems to have been well conceived; but it was evidently not a financial success, for I find that the property was mortgaged by Mr. Ropes, in June, 1835, to the Trustees of the Ministerial Fund; in December following to Benjamin Muzzey, for $200; in March, 1836, to Thaddeus Munroe, for $300; in September following to A. P. Wyman, for $300; and in May, 1837, to Calvin Smith, for $500; and that the enterprise was soon thereafter abandoned.

In 1838, the Legislature of Massachusetts passed the resolve making an appropriation for Normal Schools.

The Board of Education decided that they would be influenced to some extent as to the location of the schools by the interest shown by the people in the object.

Plymouth County was early in the field, to secure one of the schools. Wrentham and Braintree applied for Norfolk; Barre, Southbridge, and Lancaster, for Worcester; Dummer Academy at Byfield, for Essex. Concord competed with Lexington for Middlesex; and Topsfield, Worthington, New Salem, and Northfield pressed their claims. Lexington was fortunate in having at that time this building, which could be availed of. This the people offered free of rent, and in addition raised by subscription $543 towards its fitting and furnishing, and gave further pledges of assistance.

The Board of Education in their report to the Legislature say: —

"At the last meeting, on the 28th of December, we received from persons interested in the cause of education at Lexington the offer of a building well fitted for the purpose and of liberal pecuniary co-operation towards the current expenses of the institution.

"The village has all the advantages to be desired, of local situation. Great interest is manifested in its establishment in behalf of many citizens of the place; and the premises placed at the disposition of the Board are convenient and ample."

As soon as the offer made by Lexington was accepted, many alterations were made in the building: the basement was fitted for a kitchen and dining-room, the first story for the model school, the main hall for the principal school-room, and the attic story was divided into rooms for pupils.

This building was occupied by the Normal School from 1839 to 1844.

After the removal of the school, it had a curious history. For a while it was occupied by Mr. and Mrs. Waite for a boarding and day school. The school seems to have been well patronized, but without special merit. The most notable item of interest in its history is the fact that ex-Governor Robinson was a pupil; and his painstaking in all his duties and his energetic essays and declamations are well remembered by his associates. For still another while it was fitted into tenements, and rented to a considerable number of Irish tenants. Later, it was occupied as a grocery store.

April 27, 1842, Nathaniel Mulliken, for the Trustees of the Ministerial Fund, took formal possession of the property, under foreclosure of mortgages, stating in the certificate "the same being now occupied by the Board of Education for a Normal School." Two of these mortgages were assigned to Thaddeus Munroe; and the others were apparently cut out by the foreclosure, as they stand on the record undischarged.

Immediately after the purchase of the land, the Trustees of the Academy leased to Mr. Augustus, for ninety-nine years, the rent of one dollar to be paid in twenty years, a strip of land between the building and the new Bedford road, on the condition that no building should be erected on it. It will also be remembered that he sold the land for the purpose of an Academy.

The building ceasing to be used for the purpose, Mr. Augustus appears to have made some claim to it, and in 1833 assumed to convey by deed the whole property to John P. Meriam for $100, describing it as "the same tract which he sold conditionally to the Trustees of Lexington Academy to put an Academy on."

From time to time, some obstructions have been placed upon portions of the land, apparently for the purpose of maintaining the claim under this deed. And the lease and the conditions seem still to attach to the property.

To complete the chain of title, in 1866 the property was conveyed by Mrs. Rebecca Randall, of Woburn, daughter of Thaddeus Munroe, to Deacon John Field and Oliver R. Clark, and later (1868) by them to the Hancock Congregational Society.

LEXINGTON NORMAL SCHOOL.

By Miss Rebecca Viles, an Early Graduate. Read April 12, 1887.

The Normal School fills a creditable place in the history of Lexington. The Board of Education, after visiting several towns in the State, decided that Lexington was the most eligible place, and made known their wishes to the people of the town. It was an experiment; but, after much consideration, the town decided to accept their propositions. The opening, July 3, 1839, was a humble one. Only three timid female pioneers presented themselves for examination,— one from Lincoln, one from West Cambridge (now Arlington), and another from Charlestown. They occupied the building now used as the Hancock Church, which had been occupied previously for many years by a private school or academy. It has since undergone so many alterations that there is little now to suggest the old school building. Rev. Cyrus Pierce was selected as principal. In person, he was below medium height, of a slightly stooping figure, with long, black, silvered hair, parted in the middle, and brushed, painfully smooth, behind his ears, revealing a brow of indomitable will and energy. He was possessed of sterling qualities, scrupulously conscientious, never swerving from the path of duty to win the applause of others; and, though not brilliant, he gained the respect of all who came in contact with him. He had been pastor of a Unitarian society in North Reading, but came directly from Nantucket, where he taught the High School for many years, bringing with him an estimable wife, who was a great assistance to him with her hopeful spirit, and who proved a most faithful adviser to the young ladies. The principal soon won the appellation of "Father Pierce," which he deservedly sustained while connected with the school. The outlook was not very cheering at first, and the empty seats at times disheartened him; but he said, "I have put my hand to the plough, the furrow must be driven through, and the whole field turned over, before I will relinquish my effort." Soon the soil yielded to his indomitable perseverance, the horizon brightened, as each week brought new recruits from the neighboring towns and cities; and, ere the first term had closed, quite a class had joined the school. Nantucket was well represented, a place proverbial for its intellectual culture and refinement. Success now seemed assured; and the next year opened with a large class, including many from Lexington, the writer among the number, who can attest the truth of all the commendation ever bestowed upon its principal and his assistants. No one who did not know Father Pierce personally can realize the amount of work he accomplished. He never allowed himself more than five hours' sleep, attending to all his correspondence, examining and criticising each school journal, and performing the duties of janitor. He regarded no work as degrading, if well done. His personal influence over his pupils was great, and he early impressed it upon their minds that the fate of the school depended largely on the impression they made upon the public when they went out to teach.

Never was there a more earnest and self-sacrificing set of young people than those first graduates, and they realized his most sanguine expectations. Nothing sectarian was ever connected with the school, no superfluous course of instruction was instituted; but a thorough knowledge of all the English branches, including music and drawing, was insisted upon. He made a specialty of reading, and was singularly successful in teaching it; also mental arithmetic, believing that, as an exercise, it had great power to develop concentration of mind. He never accepted any half-way analysis of a question, and cancelled the word *fail* from our vocabulary. Attempting was with him synonymous with succeeding. Everything was taught with a view to imparting it to others. There was a model or experimental school, composed of children from the village, where the normal pupils were led by turns under Father Pierce's supervision to test for themselves the best methods of governing and instructing. Thus each one, when she graduated, carried with her some experience in conducting a school. This department proved a very valuable and attractive feature of the institution.

A paper was issued monthly by the students, called the *Normal Experiment*, filled with select and humorous matter, which held no mean rank in the annals of the school. As Father Pierce listened to its reading with an approving smile, and closed the exercises of the day with a subdued stroke of his bell, repeating the motto over his desk, "Live to the truth," each pupil felt its significance: it was a symbol of his own daily life. Social and intellectual development were pleasantly combined.

The "Normal Grove" (now owned by Mr. B. F. Brown)

was a part of the institution, fitted up with every convenience for healthy recreation; and many pleasant gatherings were enjoyed under the shade of its broad trees. An amusing scene occurred there at the last reunion before Father Pierce left the school. His pupils purchased a large gold pencil, and had "Live to the truth" engraved on the stone at the top. It was to be presented by one of the pupils with a little speech; but the mirthfulness of the occasion seemed to forbid a suitable time, unless it was more formal than they desired. In the mean time, Father Pierce, wishing to say a few words to his pupils, mounted a high seat, and in his stentorian voice said, "Young ladies, please give your attention a few moments," which immediately brought them around him. Suiting the action to his words, the pencil was then presented. Too much surprised for any reply, and looking like a bashful, awkward school-boy, he soon joined in the laugh he had unconsciously caused. Wise heads were interested in the success of this first Normal School. Such men as Hon. Horace Mann, Jared Sparks, and Robert Rantoul were on the Board of Education, and occasionally by their presence stimulated our advancement. They often said that, had it not been for Father Pierce, the cause of normal schools would have failed or been postponed for an indefinite period. In 1842, at the close of three successful years of teaching, he was obliged to resign. Too close application to his work demanded rest.

Rev. Samuel J. May occupied his place for two years, at the end of which time he resigned. This bright school record in Lexington was now to terminate. More money was required to meet its exigencies than the town was willing to grant. It seemed unwise to let the school go, as it promised to far more than repay the extra outlay. It had already increased the revenue of the railroad and post-office departments, bringing many visitors and residents into town; and it was sure to facilitate the intellectual development of the rising generation. However, it was not to be annihilated. West Newton came to the rescue, and gladly offered to take it, with all its liabilities. Accordingly, in 1844, it was removed there. Entire repose of body and mind had so recruited Father Pierce that he was able to resume his labors. For five years more he worked on with his wonted fidelity and success, though never so happy and contented as when in Lexington. In 1849, his health again compelled him to resign, when he received a generous donation from his friends and pupils, which enabled him to travel in Europe, the first recreation he had indulged in since 1810, when he left college. After his return in 1850, for several years he assisted in a private school in West Newton, where he continued to live until he died in 1860, after an experience of fifty years of teaching, mourned by a large circle of friends, who will always remember him as one of the most successful educators of this century. Some years after his death, several members of the first graduating class visited Mrs. Pierce at Nantucket, and laid offerings of grateful remembrance on her husband's grave. The attention was very gratifying to her; and she assured them of his life-long love and interest in his Normal children, as he often called them. In 1884, her gentle spirit joined his, leaving tender memories with many, who will ever feel the influence of this revered and worthy couple.

The building in West Newton again proved inadequate to the increasing numbers of the school; and in 1853 it was removed to Framingham, where it still remains in a very flourishing condition. Miss Ellen Hyde, a devoted and efficient teacher, is now the principal. The success of the school proves that its work was admirably adapted to the country's needs; and similar schools have since been established in Bridgewater, Westfield, Salem, Worcester, and Boston. The biennials of the graduates at Framingham are attended with much interest, which is largely due to the persevering efforts of Mrs. George Walton, a graduate and a former teacher in Lexington. Her husband is now acting as agent for the Board of Education, spending his time in the interest of the public schools of Massachusetts. In 1889 occurs the "Semi-centennial," when it is proposed to have a grand celebration of the founding of this the *first* normal school in America.

I will close by expressing the wish that it was still in old historic Lexington, a living memorial of our former educational renown.

A SKETCH OF THE LIFE AND CHARACTER OF THE LATE WILLIAM EUSTIS,

WHO DIED WHILE GOVERNOR OF MASSACHUSETTS.

Read Dec. 14, 1887, by the Rev. G. W. Porter, D.D.

One of the many illustrious names that adorn the annals of American history is that of William Eustis, who was born in Cambridge, Mass., on the tenth day of June, A.D. 1753. He was the second son of Benjamin and Elizabeth Eustis, both of whom were persons of high respectability and sterling worth. They were types of the best grade of New England character. They early espoused the cause of American independence, and were its earnest and stanch advocates and defenders in the painful struggle that issued in its establishment.

At the beginning of the Revolutionary War, they were living in Boston, where Mr. Eustis was engaged in business. But, when the town was converted into a British military camp, they removed to Lexington, in order to escape the discomforts and dangers to which all patriotic residents of Boston were exposed. Later, Mr. Eustis returned to Boston, and died there, at the age of eighty-four years, May 4, 1804, and was buried in Copp's Hill Burying-ground. His wife died twenty-nine years before in Lexington, March 30, 1775, or just twenty days before the battle of Lexington, and was buried in the old cemetery of this ancient and memorable town. As a faithful and devoted mother, she superintended the early years of her son, and by the excellence of her disposition left upon his mind impressions of her worth that never were weakened through all his life. He had the early misfortune to lose her,— a loss he never ceased to regret; and it was his earnest desire, frequently expressed, that beside her slumbering ashes his own might repose. After a lapse of fifty years, that filial wish was gratified; and the dust of mother and that of son now commingle. This wish to be buried by his mother's side was not only verbally expressed, but he carried a written request to that effect about his person during the war; and it was found in his pocket-book at the time of his death,— an evidence of filial affection and tender veneration for a mother which, I do not err in saying, is rarely found.

William's early education was obtained at the grammar school in Boston, under the celebrated Mr. John Lovell. He there displayed early promise of future eminence, and became a favorite of both the master and his usher. At the early age of fourteen years, in July, 1768, he entered Harvard University. While there, without being what is usually denominated a hard student, he was distinguished as a good classical scholar, and in token of approbation as such received a *detur digniori* from the college government. The Rev. Dr. John Eliot, of Boston, a man of uncommon worth, was both his room-mate and class-mate, for whom he ever entertained a high respect and affection. With reputation, he took his bachelor's degree at the annual commencement in 1772, on which occasion an honorable part in a Greek dialogue was assigned to him. Upon his graduation at college, he commenced the study of medicine in Boston, under Joseph Warren, M.D., subsequently known as Major-General Warren, who fell at Bunker Hill, bravely defending American liberty. Mr. Eustis's personal appearance, his polished manners, and gentlemanly address, added to his many amiable characteristics, and an intellect naturally strong and well cultivated, rendered him a favorite of his youthful friends and fellow-students, and secured for him the strong and growing attachment of his instructor. Not long after he became his pupil, Dr. Warren ventured to a friend a prophecy of his future distinction, which was literally fulfilled in a career of long and distinguished usefulness.

In the year 1774, while yet his pupil, Dr. Warren proposed an appointment to him as surgeon's mate in a British regiment stationed at Pensacola, which he offered to obtain for him through the influence of a very respectable physician in Boston. Although the situation was no small object to him at the time, yet, foreseeing the event that was coming, and the thought striking his mind that he would become the surgeon of men who might turn their arms against the colonies, he politely declined the proposal. A short time afterward, offering his services in defence of his country's threatened liberties, he caused his name to be enrolled among "the minute-men of Lexington"; and at the age of twenty-one years, in April, 1775, through the recommendation of Dr. Warren, he was made surgeon of the regiment of artillery, then at Cambridge. On the 19th of April, 1775, while Mr. Eustis was a student with General Warren, an express arrived in Boston. The general mounted his horse, called Mr. Eustis, and said: "I am going to Lexington. You go round and take care of the patients." In making the visits, the youthful physician found everything in confusion. The patriots were continually coming to the house of Dr. Warren for news; and his own mind became so inspired with patriotic ardor that, having discharged his duties to the sick, he felt that his place was at the scene of conflict. At mid-day, Lieutenant Governor Gill conveyed him to Lexington and Concord. The next day, Mr. Eustis returned to Cambridge. The American troops were fast assembling. The time of general and combined resistance to armed aggression had come. Regiments were formed. General Warren said to his youthful and patriotic pupil, "You must be surgeon of one of these regiments." His answer was: "I am too young. I expect that such men as you and Dr. Church will be surgeons, and that we shall be mates." "We have more important affairs to attend to," said the general; "and you have seen more practice than most of these gentlemen from the country." Accordingly, Mr. Eustis was made surgeon.

Accidental circumstances sometimes form the character, or rather develop those traits of it which otherwise had slept in embryo. It was so now with Dr. Eustis. His introduction to his new situation elicited powers of which till now he himself was perhaps unconscious.

Dr. Eustis was in the battle of Bunker Hill, and served by the side of his distinguished friend, the patriotic and valorous Warren. After the battle, the wounded were brought to the old Vassall House in Cambridge, and placed under the special care of Dr. Eustis and other surgeons. Dr. Eustis, then but twenty-one years of age, was senior surgeon in the Camp Hospital. He wrote as follows after the battle: "I will assist to the utmost of my ability in dressing the wounded. I see their distress, feel for them, and will relieve them in any way in my power."

Dr. Eustis continued to hold the office of physician and surgeon, either regimental or general, throughout the Revolutionary War. Subsequently, he resigned, and resumed the practice of medicine in Boston, where he attained eminence and success in his profession.

Dr. Eustis was called from the practice of medicine and the enjoyment of social life, which he so highly adorned, to serve the State that he had contributed so largely to make free and independent. While still young, he was elected to the legislature of his native State. He served a number of years in the Governor's Council. For a much longer time, he represented Massachusetts in the United States Congress. On the inauguration of James Madison as President of the United States, 1809, he was appointed Secretary of War, which position he held until he was appointed Minister Plenipotentiary to the Court of the Hague, Mr. Alexander Everett being Secretary of Legation.

In the year 1810, Dr. Eustis married Caroline, daughter of Judge Woodbury and Sarah Sherborn Langdon, of Portsmouth, N.H., a lady remarkable for her beauty, accomplishments, amiable characteristics, and conversational powers. While residing abroad, Dr. and Mrs. Eustis formed many distinguished acquaintances, which were long maintained by correspondence.

Dr. Eustis's residence on the Continent gave him the opportunity of personal intercourse with his old friend and companion in arms, General Lafayette. Between these two gentlemen there existed a warm and life-long friendship, cemented by sharing common dangers and by united efforts in the cause of our national freedom.

On the return of Mr. Eustis to his native State in 1819,

he purchased the Shirley mansion in Roxbury, built by the Colonial Governor Shirley about the year 1750. This house, modelled after the English manor house of the seventeenth and eighteenth centuries, was of magnificent proportions, elaborately and expensively constructed, and situated in highly ornamented and picturesque grounds. During its occupancy by Mr. Eustis, it was the scene of a generous and elegant hospitality, and many distinguished persons of both native and foreign birth were welcomed to its open portals and entertained within its ample walls. After the death of Governor Eustis, his widow continued to occupy the mansion until her death in 1865, a period of forty years. This elegant old house still stands, it having been removed after Madam Eustis's death, under the pressure of local enterprise, a short distance from its original site.

In the year 1820, Mr. Eustis was again elected to Congress, and represented Massachusetts in the House of Representatives from 1820 to 1823, when he was chosen Chief Magistrate of the Commonwealth as successor to Governor Brooks. Governor Eustis was deservedly popular as Chief Magistrate. His policy was liberal, and his administration was efficient. He was not the scheming, partisan politician, but the broad-minded, thoughtful, and patriotic statesman.

In August, 1824, on the occasion of the visit of the Marquis de Lafayette to the United States as guest of the republic, he was entertained by Governor Eustis at his residence in Roxbury. The marquis was received by a cavalcade of citizens, the bells were rung, while salvos of artillery and a discharge of rockets evinced the general enthusiasm and the heartiness of the welcome. A grand entertainment was given by the governor, at which were present, among other distinguished gentlemen, ex-Governor Brooks and General Dearborn, both of whom had served with distinction in the army. After making a tour through the United States, Lafayette returned to Roxbury, where he passed the night of the 16th of June, 1825. The next morning he was escorted to Bunker Hill, where, on the fiftieth anniversary of the battle, he assisted in laying the corner-stone of the monument. Governor Eustis was elected a second time to fill the gubernatorial chair; but he was not permitted to complete the allotted time of service. On the first day of February, 1825, he left his home in Roxbury for the council chamber in Boston, in his usual health. At the moment of departure, he took a pen, and wrote on a slip of paper these words, "February 1st, '25, when certainly I was alive," and, accompanied by a kiss, gave it to a favorite niece, then a child, and still living. He never returned to his home alive. He took a cold, which resulted in an attack of pneumonia, that terminated fatally in Boston on the 6th of February, 1825. Thus suddenly was his career of usefulness cut short by the great destroyer. His death caused universal sorrow, and was followed by a public funeral of unusual solemnity,— an event still remembered by the older residents of Boston and vicinity. His interment took place in the old cemetery in Lexington. The monument erected over his grave bears the following inscription on the face, composed by his friend, the Hon. Edward Everett:—

"Here lies the body of His Excellency, William Eustis, who was born in Cambridge June 10th A.D. 1753 and died in Boston Feb'y 6th, 1825.

"He served his country as a surgeon through the Revolutionary War — in her political affairs he subsequently took an active lead — he successively filled the distinguished places of Secretary of War, Envoy Extraordinary and Minister Plenipotentiary at the court of the Netherlands, Representative to Congress, and Governor of the commonwealth of Massachusetts."

On the reverse : —

"To the honored and beloved memory of a Revolutionary Patriot, a servant of his country in its highest trusts, a friend of his country in its darkest hours, an eloquent orator, a practical statesman, a dutiful son, an affectionate husband, this monument is erected by his mourning widow Caroline Langdon Eustis.

"He hastened to his country's service on the eventful morning of the 19th of April, 1775, and here within the precincts hallowed by the blood which was shed that day, after an honorable and useful life, he rests in peace and hope, conformably to his last wish, by his mother's side.

" How sweetly sink the brave to rest,
With all their country's honors blest!"

In closing this sketch, I will relate one or two incidents in his life while a surgeon in the Revolutionary army.

At a dark period of the war, when resources for supporting the army or maintaining the hospitals were nearly exhausted, and it became a question of the most painful interest whence they were to be replenished, Dr. Eustis, with characteristic generosity and patriotism, assumed the entire expense for many months of the hospital under his charge.

In this connection, I may add, like most Revolutionary officers, he returned poor from the army. Speaking of this circumstance, he said, "With but a single coat, four shirts, and one pair of woollen stockings, in the hard winter of 1780, I was yet one of the happiest men on earth."

COLONEL FRANCIS FAULKNER AND THE BATTLE OF LEXINGTON.

PORTIONS OF A PAPER READ BY REV. CYRUS HAMLIN, D.D., MAY 13, 1886.

COLONEL FRANCIS FAULKNER, of Acton, was my grandfather on the maternal side. His eldest son, Francis, Jr., was in his sixteenth year at the battle of Lexington.

Although most of our neighbors in my native place, Waterford, Maine, were Revolutionary soldiers, or brothers of such, it was from Uncle Francis that I received the most vivid account of the great day of Lexington.

I was then about thirteen or fourteen. It was during his first remembered visit to Maine, though I had afterward opportunities to talk with him when I had visited these scenes myself.

Before speaking of the family history, I will give the substance of his narration. Some of the minute events which gave a dramatic interest are of course forgotten, but most of them were indelibly impressed upon my memory. I had seen soldiers from Saratoga and Yorktown, but never from Lexington and Concord. Those names were sacred, separated from all others, and belonged rather to the Holy Land.

Francis, Jr., said he was lying awake early in the morning of the 19th of April, 1775, no one yet moving, and listening to the clatter of a horse's feet drawing nearer and nearer. Suddenly he leaped from his bed, ran to his father's room, and cried out,—

"Father, there's a horse coming on the full run; and he's bringing news!"

His father, Colonel Francis, already had on his pantaloons and his gun in his hand. The fleet horseman wheeled across the bridge and up to the house, and shouted:—

"Rouse your minute-men, Mr. Faulkner! The British are marching on Lexington and Concord!" And away he went to speed on the news.

Mr. Faulkner, without stopping to dress, fired three times, as fast as he could load and fire, that being the preconcerted signal to call out the minute-men. As chairman of the Committee of Safety and colonel of the Middlesex Regiment of Militia, the men were to assemble at his house.

Almost immediately a neighbor repeated the signal, and the boy Francis listened with breathless interest to hear the signal guns grow fainter and fainter off in the distant farm-houses. Signal fires were also lighted, and every house awoke from its slumbers to the terrors of war.

By this time the family were all up in the greatest commotion, the younger children crying because the British would come and kill them all.

Very soon the minute-men began to come in, every one with his gun, powder-horn, pouch of bullets, and a piece of bread and cheese,— the only breakfast he proposed to make before meeting the enemy of his country. Some came hurrying in with their wives and children, in the greatest excitement, to get more certain news and to know what was to be done. Captain Davis came down with some of his men, and said he would march as soon as thirty should come in.

In the mean time they were busy driving down stakes on the lawn and hanging kettles for cooking the soldiers' dinner. They brought from the houses beef and pork, potatoes and cabbages. The women would cook the dinner, and some of the elder boys — of whom Francis, Jr., was one — were designated to bring it along, packed in saddle-bags.

By the time these preliminaries for dinner were made, Captain Davis formed his men, and they marched amid the prayers and tears of their families. Colonel Faulkner accompanied them, to take command of the Middlesex Regiment, as the other companies would come in at Concord.

Uncle Francis, the boy, waited with great impatience for the dinner to be cooked and packed. Every woman wanted to prepare the dinner, complete and separate, for her husband or sons. But after much discussion it was agreed to pack all the beef, pork, bread, and vegetables in quantity, each kind by itself, and let the men themselves divide it. At length, after some hours of talking and boiling and packing, the horses were loaded and the boys started off. I asked Uncle Francis why in the world they did not take a wagon, and one horse would be enough for the whole. Didn't they know enough to do that?

"Oh, yes, my son: they knew too much to do that. The British soldiers might have the road. If we saw a 'red-coat,' we were told to give him a wide berth, or he might get us and our dinners. We could quickly topple over a stone wall, or take out a few rails, and escape through the fields and find our men wherever they might be."

Thus mounted, the boys pushed on to Concord. They met with no one to give them news. Every house was deserted or waiting in the greatest anxiety. Firing had been heard, and that was all that they knew. Everybody had gone; nobody had returned.

Arrived at Concord, they learned that the British had retreated; that Captain Davis and Mr. Hosmer were killed, and Mr. Heywood mortally wounded,—all of them Acton neighbors. But the British were on the run for Boston, and the minute-men were pressing them on both sides of the road and would kill or capture them all.

The boys pressed on toward Lexington with their dinners. Francis was feeling very badly that three of their own townsmen were already killed and perhaps his own father had fallen. As they rode along, he saw a man, wounded or dead, lying beside a wall in the field.

"O boys, that is my father!" he cried, and, jumping off his horse, ran to him. It was a dreadful sight to the boy. He had never seen death in such bloody and ghastly form before. But it was not his father, and he returned with the somewhat cheerful declaration, "That's not my father, boys; and I don't know who it is."

Pursuing their way toward Lexington, they found the road deserted and could learn but little. The women and children had run away, and the men had gone after the British. Confusion, destruction, and signs of rapid flight everywhere! Again and again did they see a dead body with fear and trembling.

As they approached Lexington, they heard the report of cannon and learned that re-enforcements had come out from Boston and stopped the flight.

Here, after wandering to right and left and making

many inquiries, they found the Acton men, who were glad of their dinner. They were watching the British, out of range of their muskets and the cannon they had ceased to fear. The balls did no execution except upon the earth for the minute-men avoided exposing themselves, or, if exposed, they changed their position too quickly to allow the enemy to get the range.

To the great surprise of the boy, he found the Acton men in the highest spirits. They had made the "red-coats" run for their lives; they had shot them down; they had seen them fall; they had avenged upon the murderers the death of the Acton men tenfold, and would destroy them all before they could get to Boston. The minute-men were coming in on all sides. They ridiculed the cannon that hurt nobody and the marksmanship of the soldiers, who, they said, fired by guess. They only wished they had the powder and ball the "red-coats" wasted. The boy wondered greatly to find his father and all the Acton men full of confidence and fight. The colonel was organizing his regiment to work upon the flank of the enemy as soon as he should move again for Boston.

The boys, having delivered the dinners, were all sent back to tell the anxious families the news, every one of them wishing he could get a shot at the murderous British. Indignation filled every heart.

Many stories were afterward told about the terror and flight of families from the empty houses. One woman, finding the British were really approaching and close at hand, caught up her child and ran nearly a mile to a house off the road. When she arrived, out of breath and ready to sink down, she found, to her horror, that she had taken the old cat. She flew back with still swifter steps, and was overjoyed to find her child uninjured. It should be remembered to the credit of the English army that it spared the life of an unprotected infant. To have killed it would have been in keeping with many of their atrocities on that memorable day.

The boys returned at night to assure the waiting mothers and sisters that their victory was complete, and not a minute-man would turn back so long as there was a prospect of destroying the British invaders.

Colonel Faulkner followed them and harassed their flank until they reached Cambridge and were under the protection of the fleet on Charles River.

From that day forward the boy Francis was forced into sudden manhood. His father was most of the time away from home, involved in the great contest; and, as the eldest of the children and naturally fearless and ambitious, he dashed into a manhood that was to have nearly seventy years of great activity from that day onward.

As one object of our society is to rescue, so far as possible, the fading histories of those Revolutionary families that took an active part in the conflict of April 19, I will here sketch some of the leading facts of Colonel Faulkner's life.

For thirty-five successive years he was chosen town clerk of Acton, and the records are kept with neatness, clearness, and order. He was a member of the Provincial Congress of 1774, and a representative to the General Court in 1783–85. In his military life after Lexington and Concord, he served under Washington on Dorchester Heights; and Francis, Jr., often went thither to carry clothes and provisions. He recalled, with special interest, the admiration he had of his father in his new uniform and mounted on his white horse. Colonel Faulkner also served under Gates at Saratoga. He guarded the British prisoners surrendered by Burgoyne, and conducted them to Cambridge. He had the satisfaction of leading the enemies of his country as prisoners over the same ground where they had brutally opened the war and where, two and a half years before, he had helped pursue them in ignominious flight to the shelter of their fleet.

I do not find any record of further military service except that in Shattuck's History of Concord it is said that "Lieut.-Colonel Francis Faulkner and Capt. Simon Hunt were in the battle of White Plains."

He was for many years a justice of the peace and one of the selectmen of his town and a deacon of the church. He died in 1805, honored and lamented. In the History of Acton, after stating the chief facts of his life, it is said: "In all places he exhibited the character of a gentleman of sound judgment, of cultivated mind, and of good, practical common sense. He was a courageous military officer, an able legislator, an impartial justice, and an exemplary Christian."

LEXINGTON IN 1775 AND IN 1861.

READ BY WALTER SAMPSON, MARCH 12, 1889.

APRIL 19, 1775, began a struggle which lasted for seven long years, ending with the surrender of Cornwallis at Yorktown, when these colonies of Great Britain became free and independent. It seemed as if nothing was lacking for the prosperity and happiness of the people of the United States. But Yorktown, far from being the end, was but the beginning of the end.

Here were thirteen confederacies, linked together by a weak bond,— the Articles of Confederation,— practically powerless to protect themselves not only from foreign invasion, but possibly from one another, should any serious internal difficulty arise. Finally, by discussions and compromises, they found a rock on which all could stand, brought into being the Federal Constitution, and thus concluded another great epoch in the history of our country. This was progress; but, like Yorktown, it was but the beginning of the end.

It had been asserted by the great minds of the Old World that, though the United States were very prosperous and apparently very strong, in reality they were the reverse; that, naturally, our ship of State would sail serenely in fair weather, but that a government of the people could not stand any severe storm; that, should civil dissensions eventually plunge this country into war, she could not stand the pressure, but would meet a fate which seemed to them inevitable. We were looked upon as a feeble power, and, in fact, hardly dared to ask ourselves if we could survive any great trial. Such a trial was near at hand. The question whether "this government," to quote the words of Lincoln, "could endure half slave and half free," must eventually come to a settlement. Careful manœuvrings had gone on for years,— the admission first of a slave, then of a free State, each side watching for an advantage, the South in the ascendency, but the North growing stronger and more determined, until at last, upon the election of Lincoln, the South endeavored to set up and maintain a government of her own.

That brought us face to face with the issue; and, as the blood shed on Lexington Common on the 19th of April, 1775, was the beginning of the first chapter in the history of a perfect Union, so the New England blood spilled in the streets of Baltimore on the 19th of April, 1861, marked the beginning of the last, and made the 19th of April doubly honored and doubly sacred. I feel that to hail from Middlesex County, the home of Parker and Munroe in 1775, and Ladd and Whitney in 1861, is an honor not to be lightly regarded.

It is a matter of great interest to know what part Lexington took in the war which united us beyond the possibility of separation. Some may think the subject is too hackneyed. But a large proportion of the young members of this society have scant recollection of our Civil War; and to many others, including myself, born at or near its close, it is as strange a story as the Revolution itself.

The great heroes of our fathers were Washington, Green, Lafayette, Knox; while our heroes are Lincoln, Grant, Sherman, Sheridan, Thomas, and Meade. *They* were wont to hold in highest veneration the names of Hancock, Otis, Quincy, and Adams; while *we* hold in no less esteem the men who reflected credit on the old Bay State in the war for the Union. We rejoice that we are members of the same Commonwealth that produced Andrew, Sumner, Wilson, Butler, and Banks.

At a meeting of the town, held April 30, 1861, the following resolutions were adopted: —

WHEREAS an insurrection exists in several States of this Union, and the insurgents have trampled upon the laws, Constitution, and property, and insulted the flag of the country by commencing war upon the brave troops and loyal citizens who rested in its folds, and are now threatening the capital of the country; and

WHEREAS the President of the United States, in obedience to his oath of office and the requirements of the laws, has called upon the States to furnish certain quotas to sustain the Constitution and the laws, to defend the capital of the country and protect the property and lives of our citizens,— be it

Resolved, That it is the duty of all good citizens to obey the call of the Government and flock to the standard of our country, and thus preserve our glorious Constitution, under which we have enjoyed greater blessings than have fallen to the lot of any other people; and

That to show our devotion to our institutions, and our just appreciation of the patriotism of the young men who are willing to respond to their country's call, it is

Voted, That a sum not exceeding $4,000 (four thousand dollars) be appropriated from any money in the treasury, to be expended under the direction of a committee of ten (10), for the purpose of clothing and otherwise encouraging the gallant men who may enter the service, and for the support of the families of those who may have families dependent on them for their labor, during the period for which they were called into service.

The committee of ten was as follows: Charles Tidd, Loring S. Pierce, William D. Phelps, Sylvanus W. Smith, Charles K. Tucker, William W. Keith, Winslow Wellington, Eli Simonds, Reuben W. Reed, and Charles Hudson.

Voted, That the committee be instructed to pay $10 (ten) per month for single men without any families, and $15 to men with families.

To further this object, it was voted to reconsider the vote whereby the town voted to pay $2,000 toward the payment of the town debt.

The committee subsequently reported for clothing, drilling, aid to two families, and other items, that they had expended the sum of $579.94.

July 19, 1862, the town voted a bounty of $100 to every soldier, and afterwards increased it to $200.

Lexington always kept her quota full, and at the end of the war had nine more men in the field than she was obliged to send. In addition to these sums, various individuals contributed $4,000 or thereabouts. Mr. Leonard A. Saville was town treasurer at the close of the war; and at the time when the town, after several unsuccessful attempts, finally voted to reimburse these parties, directing him as treasurer to proceed to do so, which he did, a number of citizens who were not in sweet accord with the putting down of the Rebellion, especially when their pocket-books were touched, paid their taxes under protest. But a case occurred where another town had done the same thing, under nearly similar circumstances; and, on the matter being brought to the Supreme Court, it was decided that the treasurer of that town and his bondsmen were personally liable. However, nothing came of it;

but it shows how carefully the financial affairs of a town must be managed, in order to avert legal difficulties of various kinds.

It would weary you to detail the votes passed, money raised and expended, and patriotic measures adopted during the four years; but those I have given you will serve as examples. Suffice to say, the cost to Lexington for the maintenance of her quota and all matters connected therewith was about $27,000.

I will here enumerate the names of the direct descendants of those who fought on the Common on the morning of the 19th of April, 1775, who enlisted in the war of the Rebellion: —

Edward T. Chandler, Lexington's first volunteer, enlisted four days after the attack on Fort Sumter, in 3d Regiment, Company C, for three months, and re-enlisted for three years in the 22d Massachusetts Regiment, and was wounded near the Wilderness, May, 1864.

His brother, Samuel E. Chandler, who enlisted in the 5th Regiment, Company K, for three months, was wounded, taken prisoner, and confined in Richmond. Upon his release in February, 1862, he was met on his return home at the Arlington line, escorted through the town, and presented with a gold watch by its citizens. He afterwards re-enlisted for three years.

Joseph Chandler, another brother, was in the army. All were descendants of John Chandler and Amos Muzzey.

Mr. Franklin V. Butters, a fellow-member of this society, descended from Joel Viles; Joseph H. P., Charles A., and Alexander Fiske, descendants of Dr. Joseph Fiske; Charles H. Fiske, descendant of "Fifer David

Fiske," — all were in the war; and the latter gave his life, that the nation might live, on the field of Antietam.

Besides the Chandler brothers, Amos Muzzey had three other descendants who were Lexington soldiers. It seems hard to realize that our fellow-townsman, George E. Muzzey, and his brother, Major Loring W. Muzzey, both respected citizens, now rounding off a half-century of life, could ever have been boys in blue; but the records so declare. Both were members of the famous Webster Regiment, otherwise known as the 12th Massachusetts; and both by successive promotions reached the ranks of First Lieutenant and Major respectively.

Charles O. Muzzey, another brother, was in the naval service, and was killed by the explosion of a torpedo in Charleston Harbor, while on the steamer "Housatonic," Feb. 18, 1864.

Windsor Smith and George H. Smith, descendants of Josiah Smith, and Charles Cutler, descendant of Thomas Cutler, died of disease contracted in the service. Cyrus M. and Alfred D. Cutler, also descendants of Thomas Cutler, and Charles B. Harrington, descendant of Robert Munroe and Daniel Harrington, died in the service. George D. Harrington, brother of Charles, our respected fellow-citizen and former Commander of the Grand Army Post of Lexington, was also in the service.

In the same regiment with Cyrus Cutler and George D. Harrington was a young man who was a great favorite for his gentlemanly demeanor and nobility of character. Every one who knew him speaks well of Joseph Simonds, son of Mr. Joseph F. Simonds. He enlisted September, 1861, in the 22d Regiment, for three years, but was severely wounded at Malvern Hill, and died from the effects of his wounds soon after. The loss to posterity occasioned by the death of thousands of men of the stamp of Joseph Simonds cannot indeed be estimated. He was a descendant of Joseph Simonds and Joel Viles, minutemen in Captain Parker's Company.

Captain John Parker had a great-grandson in the person of Charles M. Parker, a member of this society, who did his share towards the preservation of that Union the first blow for which was struck by his illustrious ancestor. He enlisted in the 24th Regiment. While he was at the front, his mother did her share at home. She was always a central figure in the sewing-society; and I have often heard the older members of my family tell how she would purchase a large side of leather at Waltham, a heavy and clumsy bundle for a woman to handle, and carry it up to the sewing-room from her sleigh or wagon, as easily as though it were feathers,—the leather being used to make extra soles for the soldiers' boots. If any of you should ever meet her, you will find a keen, vigorous old lady, well up to the times, and one whom you might well believe would speed her sons to battle for freedom, without hesitation or question.

Charles L. Tidd, descendant of John Tidd, our friend and townsman, Mr. Everett S. Locke, descendant of Amos Locke, Grovenor A. Page, a descendant of the Harringtons and Munroes, and his cousins William C. and Thaddeus Page, and perhaps others not recorded, form a list of great interest.

In this connection, I would recall the names of two direct descendants of the Revolutionary sires that fell on the Common on the morning of April 19th, who have not only reflected upon Lexington the honor which belongs to all her sons in the War of the Rebellion, but who have since achieved distinction throughout the Commonwealth in perpetuating that military spirit which has proved the nation's safety in her hour of danger.

George H. Patch, a descendant of Nathan Munroe, is an example of what a man can make of himself. Beginning life under circumstances peculiarly discouraging, he worked his way to success through difficulties which would have broken down a weaker will, a purpose less determined, or the high ambition of a nature less honorable and incorruptible. "A Grand Army man," said ex-Governor Robinson, "belongs to a peculiarly exclusive association; for blood is the one qualification for admission, and it is therefore the most aristocratic body, in the true sense of the word, that can exist." These ringing words of one who has himself reflected great credit on Lexington we all indorse.

The sudden death of Commander Patch, in the summer of 1887, was a shock to the Commonwealth. As a Lexington boy, I attended the funeral in the town of Framingham, Mass., and had an opportunity to observe the esteem in which he was held, not only by his military comrades, but by his former associates, railroad and journalistic. Prominent among the military bodies on that occasion was the now famous regiment which is the pride of Massachusetts, the one selected to do her honor on all important occasions.

No casual observer can form any estimate of the labor, time, and trouble required for the establishment of such a regiment. None but a soldier can form any idea of the great achievements in military tactics accomplished by Austin Clark Wellington, the commander, a descendant of

Timothy Wellington, a Lexingtonian by birth, and for many years a resident of this town. He attained the rank of First Lieutenant in the 38th Massachusetts Regiment during the Rebellion, and in the State Militia commanded a company of the 1st Regiment, and rose by successive promotions to be its Colonel. I may safely say that he made the regiment what it is. Gentlemanly, courteous, beloved by all who knew him, the youngest among us will be palsied and gray before the name of Colonel Wellington will have passed into oblivion. I would state here that, had he lived, arrangements had been made on the occasion of the 115th Anniversary of the Battle of Lexington, in 1890, for the entire 1st Regiment, under his leadership, to be present, and reproduce by a sham battle the scenes in which his ancestors participated. Colonel Austin C. Wellington had five cousins, sons of Horatio and T. W. Wellington, who were in the service.

By reason of previous service in affairs of State and his well-known judgment in municipal matters, Hon. Charles Hudson was pre-eminently qualified to be the town's adviser and counsellor in time of difficulty. Up to 1862, he was on the Board of Selectmen; but, having been appointed to the office of United States Assessor, he found his time too much occupied to fill the duties of both positions. His advice was always readily sought and gladly given.

Webster Smith, the present Chairman of the Board, was Selectman during the whole of that period; and he, with Hammon Reed and William H. Smith, brother of George O. Smith, formed the Board for the balance of the war. Their administration was wise and efficient. The town thought well of their service; and, at the close of the war, a vote of thanks was given Mr. Reed, as Chairman of the Board, for the able manner in which he had discharged his duties.

The churches at this time were nearly all in a somewhat unsettled state, with the exception of the First Congregational, which had for its pastor a man who was indeed a true patriot, Rev. Leonard J. Livermore. His labors in behalf of the town during the Rebellion can only be appreciated by those who were living here at that time. I judge from all I can gather that he in a measure filled the place of Jonas Clarke of Revolutionary days. During the war, two of his sermons were published by request.

Though I did not purpose to mention any but direct descendants of Revolutionary soldiers, yet I cannot forbear to allude to a lady whose labors in behalf of the soldiers were second only to those of the soldiers themselves, in devotion to the Union,— Mrs. Mary P. Olnhausen, a daughter of Elias Phinney, Esq. From 1862 to 1865, she served as a hospital nurse at Alexandria, Morehead City, Beaufort, and Smithville, N.C. She made for herself a very high reputation in the service. To quote from Mr. Hudson's account of her in his history: "We naturally extol the heroism of the gallant soldier who promptly faces danger on the field of battle; but it requires as much moral courage and as much self-sacrifice to brave the diseases of the hospital as it does to face the enemy on the field."

Lexington had two well-equipped sewing-societies, which kept the soldiers at the front supplied with everything needful for their comfort. It was the custom all over the country for young ladies to enclose a slip of paper in some of the garments they made, bearing their names.

The soldier receiving it would immediately write a letter in return. One of our Lexington girls, an aunt of mine, had a flourishing correspondence for some time with one of them. A few years ago, he was again heard from. He is now a sedate, elderly man, living somewhere in the Western country. In another case of that kind in our town, the lady, not caring to continue writing to an entire stranger after the war, requested that the correspondence should cease; and accordingly it was dropped. In a few years she died, and the matter was forgotten by her relatives. The soldier went into civil life, and probably forgot it, too. But he was detailed in the guard of honor at General Grant's funeral in 1885; and, naturally enough, the memory of the war came back to him, bringing recollection of his former correspondent. He then sat down and wrote to her address at Lexington. The letter was opened by her relatives, who remembered the man's name, and who sent an answer, telling him the circumstances. Some correspondence ensued, and there the matter rested. But on Memorial Day, two years ago, he wrote to a member of our Grand Army Post, requesting that her grave be decorated at his expense, which was done.

We honor the patriots who fought at Lexington, Bunker Hill, Saratoga, Yorktown, and on the other battle-fields of the Revolution. Their memories are enshrined in the hearts of a grateful posterity; and their heroic deeds will be rehearsed in story and song as long as this nation shall remain free and independent. But, however we may honor the one who builds the structure, surely he who bravely defends it from attack is entitled to equal consideration and esteem.

The heroic defenders of the Union will not be with us

much longer. The malaria caught in Southern swamps and prisons, the wounds received in many a hard-fought battle, are fast doing their work, and causing them to fall short of a green old age.

Let us keep the pledges we made to them, and remember that the same spirit animated the men on Lexington Common and in the streets of Baltimore, at Saratoga and Gettysburg, at Yorktown and Appomattox.

By paying them their just dues we prove that we possess something of the spirit of 1775 and 1861.

APPENDIX.

THE SECOND MEETING-HOUSE IN LEXINGTON,

ERECTED BY THE TOWN IN 1714.

THE cost of this building appears to have been about £500 sterling. The town appropriated £416 when it was first voted to erect it. Afterwards, permission was given individuals to increase the height "four feet upward" at their own expense, in order to add a second gallery. This was accordingly done, but the gallery was not finished when the meeting-house was built. Two years afterwards, the town voted to pay Joseph Merriam £54, 12s., "when the uppermost gallery in the new meeting house is finished"; but not until 1722 is this bill finally paid, which seems to indicate that the building was not completed until about that date. There is no account of a service of dedication, but "Oct. 17, 1714, was the first Sabbath day that we did mette in the new meeting house," as the town clerk has recorded. The upper gallery was probably used originally for seats for the town paupers and the slaves. Here also the town's powder was kept, and here two of the minute-men had come to get a supply when the house was surrounded by the British soldiers on the morning of the 19th of April, one of whom, Caleb Harrington, was killed in attempting to escape.

The arrangement of pews and benches is shown in the plate on page 16, the only pews being those built by individuals against the walls, who bought the spaces for them from the town. The benches were for the use of all others of the townspeople, and on these the place of each person was assigned by a committee chosen by the town for "seating the meeting house." Here they were placed according to their age and their taxable property, the old people having the front seats, and the men and women seated on opposite sides of the central aisle. That there might be no mistake in regard to their rightful positions, the people were ordered "to bring in their ages to the selectmen" before a given date. When there was a reseating of the meeting-house, the committee was instructed "not to degrade any person." The children were probably placed on the rear benches, excepting those sitting with their parents in the pews, "where they could be inspected" by the tithingmen appointed to keep order. In the first meeting-house probably there were no pews, but only benches.

SOME FACTS RELATING TO THE THIRD MEETING-HOUSE IN LEXINGTON,

BUILT BY THE TOWN IN 1794.

No dimensions of the building are found upon the records; but Mr. Charles A. Wellington, to whom we are indebted for the plan of the interior on pages 28 and 29, drawn from such data as he was able to gather, has obtained much information regarding the size and appearance of this ancient edifice by diligent inquiry among those who best remember it. We have, therefore, a very accurate representation of the pulpit, pews, aisles, and porches of this meeting-house, reproduced by his painstaking care and skill. From this information, we know that it was about seventy feet in length and between forty and fifty feet in width. At first, a space in front of the pulpit was filled with rows of seats extending on either side of the broad aisle to the side aisles; but afterward these were removed, and pews built in their place. Thus the entire floor of the house was devoted to pews, fifty-eight in number, which were sold at auction and bought by individuals. The pews against the walls on the four sides were raised six inches above the aisles, and the seats in all the pews were lifted up in prayer-time, that people might stand more easily. At the conclusion of the prayer, they were let down with a *bang*, much to the amusement of the children. The pulpit was raised about eight feet above the floor, and was reached by stairs on each side, which turned at the top, where a door opened into it. The front of the pulpit was circular between the stairs and finished downward, in shape like the end of a melon. Under the pulpit in front were the deacons' seats, and above it was a sounding-board directly over the preacher's head. This was in octagon form, and about five inches in thickness, ornamented with filigree work around the edges, and the under side, as seen from below, covered with red damask drawn to the centre. It was suspended by an iron rod from the ceiling, twisted in imitation of a rope, and the whole painted white, with streaks of gold. The pulpit was also painted white; but, with these exceptions, the interior was in the natural color of the wood. Behind the pulpit was a window with a red damask curtain drawn in flutes, and under it the seat finished into the wall, also covered with red damask. The pews were panelled, and finished above the panel-work with a rail about ten inches from the top, filled in with upright turned spindles, which the children delighted to turn and make them squeak; a misdemeanor for which they often received a tap on the head from some older and more devout member of the family. In the wall pews, the sills of the windows came just above the backs of the seats, and children were sometimes seated on them. One man remembers sitting there when a boy and counting the teams that passed by in the road toward Lowell. There were porches at the three outside doors. That at the door looking down Main Street was about thirteen feet by ten, and had a bookcase containing the Sunday-school library on the right hand of the entrance, and on the left were the stairs leading to the gallery. A porch of the same dimensions, with stairs to the gallery, was over the door toward Monument Street. On the front of the meeting-house, toward the Buckman tavern, or Merriam House, was a porch and the bell-tower. This porch had three outside doors, a large one in front and a smaller one on each side. On the left of the front door were stairs leading to the gallery, which had two turns, and filled the whole space between the front and side doors. The bell-rope usually lay in the middle of this porch on the floor, nicely coiled. A window between this porch and the interior of the house, having but one pane of glass, allowed the bell ringer to see the minister enter the pulpit, when he was to stop tolling the bell.

A spacious gallery extended around three sides of the house. It had a row of pews against the wall and three rows of seats on each side inclining toward the front: those opposite the pulpit were occupied by the singers, who stood behind red curtains hung on iron rods. The gallery front, as seen from below, was finished in horizontal panelling; and the top had a width of eight or ten inches, whereon daring boys used to run sometimes during the intermission on Sundays. The town paupers sat in the gallery seats on the west side of the house, and probably the colored people, also, though there had ceased to be any slaves in Massachusetts before this house was built. The gallery was supported by six fluted columns placed in the pews below. The ceiling and the walls of the house were roughly plastered.

Outside of the meeting-house in front was a row of hewn stone posts with a chain running over the top, and horse-blocks were originally placed at the porches for the convenience of those who rode on horseback or in wagons. It is related that on one occasion a woman, having tied her horse to a post, stooped down to pass under the chain, when the horse caught her bonnet in his mouth, and appropriated it for his noon-day meal.

Captain John Underwood is remembered as the leader of the choir, and Josiah Smith as his successor. A big bass-viol furnished the instrumental music, and the children used to gaze with wonder upon the end that could be seen under the curtain, as they sat in the pews below.

This being the only church in the town, and the custom of attending church being universal, the roads leading toward the meeting-house are said to have been black with people on Sundays, going and returning. Boys were allowed six cents by their parents to buy a sheet of gingerbread for the Sunday lunch between services, and it was usually divided among three. The post-office was kept open for an hour at noon for the accommodation of those who came to the village only on Sundays.

In the plan of the interior of this meeting-house the names of the pew-owners and the numbers of the pews are taken from the record of the sale when the church was built, with the exception of those which were added in front of the pulpit when the long seats were removed: for these we are indebted to a later plan belonging to Mr. H. B. Sampson. Of course there were many changes in the ownership and occupancy of pews in after years. Hence the names remembered by some now living will be very different from those on the plan. But in several instances the descendants of the original proprietors occupied the same pews at the time of the reconstruction of the house in 1846. The cost of the third meeting-house is nowhere given, but the sale of pews amounted to about $7,000; and, as a considerable surplus remained over and above the cost, it could not have been far from $6,000, which represents a sum at least three times as large in purchasing and building means as the same sum to-day.

APPENDIX.

A list of pew-owners in the Third Church, with the sum paid by each person when bid off at public auction, Dec. 23, 1794: —

No.		
1.	Ebenezer Bowman, Esq.,	$174.00
2.	Ministerial pew,	
3.	John Parkhurst,	152.00
4.	Simon Winship,	151.00
5.	Joshua Reed, Jr.,	154.50
6.	Joseph Underwood,	117.00
7.	Josiah Smith,	104.00
8.	Jonathan Loring,	116.00
9.	Rufus Merriam, $\frac{1}{2}$,	75.00
"	Joshua Simonds, Jr., $\frac{1}{2}$,	75.00
10.	Jonathan Smith, Jr., $\frac{1}{2}$,	78.25
"	Jonas Stone, $\frac{1}{2}$,	78.25
11.	Abraham Smith,	106.50
12.	Isaac Stone, $\frac{1}{2}$,	58.00
"	Ebenezer Munroe, $\frac{1}{2}$,	58.00
13.	Jonas Bridge,	103.00
14.	Joel Viles,	100.00
15.	Dr. Joseph Fiske, $\frac{1}{2}$,	57.00
"	Dr. Joseph Fiske, Jr., $\frac{1}{2}$,	57.00
16.	William Tidd, $\frac{1}{2}$,	65.00
"	Nathan Chandler, $\frac{1}{2}$,	65.00
17.	Attai Estabrook,	135.00
18.	Joshua Simonds,	130.00
19.	John Muzzy,	111.00
20.	Levi Mead, $\frac{1}{2}$,	85.00
"	Josiah Mead, $\frac{1}{2}$,	85.00
21.	Captain Samuel Hastings,	130.00
22.	Captain John Mulliken,	137.50
23.	Josiah Nelson,	116.00
24.	Jonathan Harrington, $\frac{1}{2}$,	33.50
"	Jonathan Harrington, $\frac{1}{4}$,	16.75
"	Rebecca Munro, $\frac{1}{4}$,	16.75
25.	Thomas Tufts,	87.50
26.	Deacon Nathan Reed,	123.00
27.	Hammon Reed, $\frac{1}{2}$,	70.00
	Amount carried forward,	$3,221.50

APPENDIX. 135

Amount brought forward,	$3,221.50
No. 27. Hammon Reed, Jr., ½,	70.00
28. John Simonds, ½,	64.00
" Samuel Simonds, ½,	64.00
29. Captain James Brown, ½,	72.50
" Samuel Downing, ½,	72.50
30. Joseph Simonds,	113.00
31. Captain Joseph Smith,	100.00
32. Bezaleel Lawrence,	58.00
33. Thomas Lock,	106.00
34. Dr. David Fiske,	81.00
35. Benjamin Willington,	117.00
36. Captain Frances Bowman, ⅔,	75.63¼
" Charles Harrington, ⅓,	37.33¾
37. Frances Bowman,	93.50
38. Abner Pierce,	119.00
39. Benjamin Phinney,	67.00
40. Thadeus Harrington, ½,	35.50
" Joshua Swan, ½	35.50
41. Colonel William Munro,	89.00
42. Jonathan Bridge,	126.00
43. Amos Muzzy, ½,	52.00
" William Abbot, ½,	52.00
44. Deacon John Bridge,	106.00
45. Amos Marrett, Jr.,	68.00
46. James Reed,	120.50
47. Robert Moore,	78.50
48. Thomas Cutler,	87.00
49. Captain John Chandler,	151.50
50. Isaac Hastings,	146.00
51. Abijah Childs,	120.00
52. Lydia Reed, ½,	85.00
" Robert Reed, ½,	85.00
53. Amos Marrett,	143.00
54. Captain Daniel Harrington,	100.00
	$6,129.47

Six pews were afterwards put in where long seats were originally placed, but who bought them we have no means of knowing.

APPENDIX.

GALLERY PEWS.

No. 1.	Parker Emerson,	$51.00
2.	Benjamin and Oliver Willington,	27.00
3.	Jacob Robinson,	42.50
4.	Nathan Fessenden,	22.00
5.	Amos Muzzy,	19.00
6.	Nehemiah Munro,	32.00
7.	James Wyman, Jr., $\frac{1}{2}$,	15.25
"	Swithen Reed, $\frac{1}{2}$,	15.25
8.	Deacon Nathan Reed, $\frac{1}{2}$,	20.25
"	Joseph Simonds, $\frac{1}{2}$,	20.25
9.	Thomas Fessenden,	34.00
10.	William Smith, Jr.,	40.50
11.	Abijah Harrington,	46.50
12.	Nathan Dudley, $\frac{1}{2}$,	14.00
"	Nathan Culley, $\frac{1}{2}$,	14.00
13.	Benjamin Lock, Sr., $\frac{1}{2}$,	15.00
"	Joseph Munro, $\frac{1}{2}$,	15.00
14.	Abner Pierce,	39.50
15.	Widow Mary Parker, $\frac{1}{2}$,	
"	Robert Parker, $\frac{1}{2}$,	47.00
16.	Benjamin Lock, Jr.,	33.50
17.	John Parker,	57.00
18.	David Willington,	25.00
19.	Nathan Russell,	46.00
20.	Daniel Harrington, Jr.,	16.50
21.	Moses Harrington,	18.50
22.	Thomas Cutler, Jr.,	44.00
23.	Nathan Munro,	26.00
24.	Samuel Stone,	60.00
	Amount of gallery pews,	$856.50
	Amount of floor pews,	6,129.47
	Whole amount of pews sold,	$6,985.97

Besides the six subsequently added, which were valued by the town at $600.

Number of pews in the gallery, ... 24
Number of pews on the floor, ... 58

Making in all, ... 82

Besides the ministerial pew.

There are nearly one hundred different persons represented in the ownership of these pews.

Proceedings.

THE Lexington Historical Society was organized at a meeting of citizens held in the Town Hall, March 16, 1886, the following call having been previously issued: —

THE LEXINGTON HISTORICAL SOCIETY.

Dear Sir,—It is proposed to form a society in Lexington for historical research and study in matters connected with the history of the town, and of families and individuals who have been identified with it, also for suitably commemorating from year to year by appropriate services the great event which has rendered the town forever memorable in the annals of our country, the object being to perpetuate a knowledge of our local history, and to awaken and sustain new interest in the honor and good name of Lexington. For the purpose of organizing this society, a meeting will be held in the Selectmen's Room at the Town Hall, on Tuesday evening, March 16, 1886, at 7.30 o'clock, to which you are cordially invited.

(Signed)   E. G. PORTER.
                       C. A. STAPLES.

LEXINGTON, March 1, 1886.

At this meeting a paper was circulated for signatures of those who wished to become members of such a society; and eighty-four names were obtained.

Committees were chosen to prepare a constitution for the government of the Society, and to arrange appropriate exercises for the celebration of the 19th of April.

MARCH 23, 1886.

Adjourned meeting. George O. Whiting in the chair.

The constitution presented by the committee was adopted, and a committee was appointed to nominate a list of officers for the ensuing year.

APRIL 13, 1886.

Adjourned meeting. George O. Whiting in the chair.

The following officers were elected by ballot: —
President, Augustus E. Scott.
Vice-Presidents, Miss Mary E. Hudson, Matthew H. Merriam, Herbert G. Locke, William A. Tower, Miss Kate Whitman.
Treasurer, Leonard A. Saville.
Corresponding Secretary, Rev. Edward G. Porter.
Recording Secretary, Alonzo E. Locke.
Historian, Rev. Carlton A. Staples.
Custodian, Dr. Robert M. Lawrence.

Rev. E. G. Porter presented to the Society the following interesting relics, the gift of Mr. Frederick F. Hassam:
Thomas Hancock's sun dial.
Printed account of the "Bloody Butchery, etc., of April 19, 1775."
Tobacco box of Caleb Harrington.
Paul Revere's lantern.
Military order to Paymaster Ebenezer Hancock, signed by Governor Gates.
Letter to Thomas Hancock from the Messrs. Hope, bankers of Amsterdam, 1750.
Letter from Commodore Hull to Lieutenant Commander John Percival.

Rev. C. A. Staples read entertaining extracts from the old records of the town.

There had been a long-felt desire among our citizens to possess a picture preserving upon canvas the landmarks of the old battle-ground, and representing an ideal of the stand for right made thereon on the 19th of April, 1775, and the Historical Society thus early entered upon the work of procuring one. Mr. Henry Sandham, a prominent artist of Boston, had for many months been at work upon such a picture, which was believed to be fine as a work of art, and historically correct. A committee was appointed to negotiate with Mr. Sandham for his painting entitled "The Dawn of Liberty," with authority to collect funds for its purchase.

CELEBRATION OF THE ONE HUNDRED AND ELEVENTH ANNIVERSARY OF THE BATTLE OF LEXINGTON.

Commemorative services were held in the Town Hall, Sunday evening, April 18, 1886. The exercises consisted of singing by a chorus of forty voices, under the leadership of Mr. J. N. Morse, and addresses by Rev. E. G. Porter, Hon. James M. Usher, Rev. G. W. Porter, D. D., Rev. C. A. Staples, Dr. Charles W. Emerson. The morning of the 19th was ushered in by the ringing of bells and the firing of guns. In the afternoon, a children's celebration was held in the Town Hall. The following is the programme of exercises:—

1. Music. 2. Prayer, Cyrus Hamlin, D.D., L.L.D. 3. Singing. 4. Address of Welcome, Rev. E. G. Porter. 5. Singing. 6. Reading, Miss Eldridge. 7. Singing. 8. Declamation, Edward P. Merriam. 9. Recitation, Miss Bullock. 10. Singing. 11. Reading, Carleton A. Shaw. 12. Recitation, Miss Rogers. 13. Singing. 14. Declamation, David S. Muzzey. 15. Address, Rev. C. A. Staples 16. Singing. 17. Reading, Miss Eldridge. 18. Singing, "America."

MAY 11, 1886.

Regular meeting. President Scott in the chair.

The following relics were presented to the Society: —

Copy of the election sermon of Rev. Jonas Clark, preached in 1781, the year of Governor Hancock's election, from Hamilton A. Hill, Esq.

Fac-simile of the deposition of Captain John Parker, taken six days after the battle of Lexington by order of the Provincial Congress.

Bank-note engraved by Paul Revere.

Proceedings of the Bostonian Society at the annual meeting, Jan. 12, 1886.

An essay on the origin of the names of towns in Massachusetts settled prior to 1775, to which is prefixed an essay on the name of the town of Lexington, by William Henry Whitmore, 1873.

The following papers were read: On the name "Lexington," by President A. E. Scott; "Colonel Francis Faulker of Acton, a Participant in the Events of April 19, 1775," by Dr. Cyrus Hamlin.

JULY 20, 1886.

Special meeting. President Scott in the chair.

The following articles were presented to the Society:—

A cradle about one hundred and twenty-five years old and a foot-stove used in the old church, by Mr. Amos Locke.

The original drawing of the seal of the town of Lexington, with the first impress of the seal, by Rev. E. G. Porter.

Steel engraving, from painting by Copley, of Mrs. John Hancock, by Mrs. William Wales, of Dorchester.

An English coin, supposed to be a penny, dated 1775, found July 16, 1886, on the Common about where it is supposed the line of minute-men stood on April 19, 1775, by Mr. E. W. Shippee.

A brass button of antique pattern, and a small bullet, recently found on the Common.

In order to more conveniently manage the property of the Society and carry out its objects, it was deemed expedient to organize the Society as a corporation under the laws of the Commonwealth, and to this end it was voted:

"That the Council cause a corporation to be formed of as many of their number as is convenient; that the organization and by-laws conform as nearly as possible to the present organization and Constitution of the Society; and that the by-laws provide that all members of the Society shall be members of the corporation."

ORGANIZATION OF THE CORPORATION.
JULY 28, 1886.

A meeting of the subscribers to the agreement of association to form a corporation was holden this evening. The corporation was duly organized as required by statute, and the following By-laws were adopted:—

ARTICLE I.

Name.—The corporation shall be called the "Lexington Historical Society."

ARTICLE II.

Objects.—The objects of this Society shall be the study of the history of Lexington and of individuals and families identified with it, the preservation of such knowledge and of such relics as illustrate its history, and the commemoration, by fitting public services, of the event which has rendered the town forever memorable in the annals of our country.

ARTICLE III.

Membership.—All persons who are now members of the association known as the "Lexington Historical Society" shall be members of this corporation. Any person who has been nominated by the Council may be elected to membership by ballot. Each member shall pay an admission fee of one dollar ($1) and an annual assessment of fifty cents (.50) after the year of admission. Any member who for two consecutive years shall fail to pay his assessments shall cease to belong to this Society. The Society may elect honorary and corresponding members in the same manner; but such members shall have no voice in the management of the Society and shall not be subject to assessments.

Article IV.

Officers.—The officers of this Society shall be elected annually by ballot, and shall consist of a President, five Vice-Presidents, a Recording Secretary, who shall also be clerk of the corporation, a Corresponding Secretary, a Treasurer, a Custodian and an Historian, whose duties shall be those usually pertaining to such offices, and who shall be elected members of and shall together constitute a Council with the powers of Directors.

Article V.

Meetings.—The Annual Meeting of the Society shall be held on the second Tuesday evening of March.

Regular meetings shall be held on the second Tuesday evenings of October, December, February, and April.

Special meetings may be called by order of the Council. All meetings shall be called by the Clerk, by sending to each member a written or printed notice thereof by mail, post-paid, three days at least before the time of meeting, or by publishing such notice in some newspaper published in said Lexington.

At all meetings of the Society, fifteen members shall constitute a quorum for the transaction of business. Meetings of the Council shall be called by the Clerk at the request of the President, by giving to each member personal or witten notice, or by sending such notice by mail, post-paid, twenty-four hours at least before the time of meeting. Meetings of the Council at which all the members are present may be held without such notice. The President shall call meetings of the Council at the request of three members thereof. At all meetings of the Council, a majority of its members shall constitute a quorum for the transaction of business.

Article VI.

Amendments.—These By-laws may be amended by a vote of two-thirds of the members present at any regular meeting, notice of the proposed amendment being given at the preceeding meeting.

The following officers were then elected:—

President, Augustus E. Scott.

Vice-Presidents, Matthew H. Merriam, Herbert G. Locke, William A. Tower, Mary E. Hudson, Kate Whitman.

Treasurer, Leonard A. Saville.

Custodian, Dr. Robert M. Lawrence.

Historian, Rev. C. A. Staples.

Corresponding Secretary, Rev. E. G. Porter.

Recording Secretary and Clerk, Alonzo E. Locke.

PROCEEDINGS.

The committee appointed by the association to negotiate for the purchase of "The Dawn of Liberty" reported that the price of the picture was $4,000, including the cost of such photogravures of the painting as the committee might require, and that it had been arranged to present these photogravures to the subscribers. The funds in the hands of the committee were transferred to the treasurer of the corporation, and the treasurer was instructed to pay to Mr. Sandham the price named by him.

AUGUST 11, 1886.

Special meeting. The last meeting of the Society as an association was holden this evening in the Town Hall, President Scott in the chair. It was voted to transfer all the property of the association known as the Lexington Historical Society to the corporation.

A special meeting of the corporation was holden to celebrate the reception and unveiling of the painting "The Dawn of Liberty." A large audience was in attendance. The platform was finely decorated with flowers and exotic plants. The picture was hung in the alcove back of the platform.

Mr. M. H. Merriam, in behalf of the committee, made a report of the work of the committee, and presented the painting to the Society. Miss Jessie Eldridge read "Paul Revere's Ride," at the conclusion of which the painting was unveiled. The president delivered an address, receiving the painting in behalf of the Society, and thanking those who had contributed toward it. Addresses were also made by Rev. E. G. Porter and Rev. C. A. Staples.

OCTOBER 12, 1886.

Regular meeting. President Scott in the chair.

The military coat of Fifer Josiah Smith, also his commission as Master of Band, dated 1822, were presented to the Society by George H. Smith, Esq., of Waltham, Mass.

The following gifts were also received:—

"History of Dedham," from Erastus Worthington.

"Memento Mori; sacred to the Memory of George Washington," executed with pen by Nathan Chandler.

Pair of spectacles used in the eighteenth century by members of the Chandler and Tidd families, from J. Q. A. Chandler.

Rev. C. A. Staples presented the following papers:—

"Order of Services at the Installation of Rev. Jason Whitman over First Parish Church, Lexington, July 30, 1845."

"Order of Services at the Dedication of Church of First Congregational Society, Lexington, Feb. 28, 1848."

"Order of Exercises at Ordination of Rev. N. A. Staples as pastor of First Congregational Society, Lexington, Sept. 20, 1854."

Dr. R. M. Lawrence presented photographs of Buckman and Munroe Taverns taken in 1886.

The following papers were read: —

"Robert Munroe," by G. Walter Sampson.

"History of Lexington Common," by Rev. C. A. Staples.

DECEMBER 14, 1886.

Regular meeting. President Scott in the chair.

The following relics were presented to the Society: —

By Mrs. G. W. Porter, the boots and spurs of Governor William Eustis; photographic portrait of the same, and hat worn by him. Mrs. Porter loaned the Society the diplomatic coat worn by Governor Eustis.

By Mr. Walter Faxon, a heliotype of the "Battle of Lexington."

By Rev. E. G. Porter, a rolling-pin given by Jonathan Harrington to Sally the day of her marriage to Charles Ellins, Feb. 8, 1830.

By Dr. R. M. Lawrence, an autograph letter of Daniel Webster, written March, 1830, to Amos Lawrence.

By Rev. C. A. Staples, the sleeve-buttons worn by Captain John Parker and donated to the Society by Mrs. Isaac Parker.

The historian read an interesting review of the prominent events of the year, noting the formation of the Lexington Historical Society and the improvement of the Common.

The following papers were read: —

"Amos Locke," by H. G. Locke.

"Experiences of our Grandmothers, April 19, 1775," by Miss Elizabeth W. Harrington.

"The Life of the late Governor William Eustis," by Rev. G. W. Porter, D.D.

FEBRUARY 8, 1887.

Regular meeting. President Scott in the chair.

Mrs. J. Q. A. Chandler loaned the Society the wedding vest of Governor Thomas Dudley.

The following gifts were presented to the Society: —

A stamp for 2s. 6d. used under the "Stamp Act" by Dr. R. M. Lawrence.

Indenture of Agreement between Thomas Hancock and Isaac Moody, a small box made from wood taken from the old Hancock mansion dining-room, by Mr. Thomas Minns, of Boston.

The Council was instructed to take action relative to securing or saving from destruction the old house formerly of Rev. Jonas Clark.

A committee was appointed to arrange a programme for the observance of the 19th of April.

The following papers were read : —

"Matthew Bridge," by Harry W. Davis.

"John Lawrence, of Wisset, England, and Some of his Descendants," by Dr. Robert M. Lawrence.

"The First Normal School in America," by A. E. Scott.

MARCH 8, 1887.

Annual meeting. Vice-President M. H. Merriam in the chair.

The following officers were elected : —

President, Augustus E. Scott.

Vice Presidents, Matthew H. Merriam, Herbert G. Locke, George E. Muzzey, Miss Elizabeth S. Parker, Miss Elizabeth W. Harrington.

Treasurer, Leonard A. Saville.

Historian, Rev. C. A. Staples.

Corresponding Secretary, Dr. Robert M. Lawrence.

Custodian, Emory A. Mulliken.

Recording Secretary and Clerk, G. W. Sampson.

The following gifts were received : —

Copies of advertisements from Boston *Gazette* of May 12, 1766, and Feb. 13, 1769.

A valuable collection of old documents, mostly relating to the Reed family, from Miss Sarah Chandler.

A committee was appointed to take in charge the celebration of the coming 19th of April.

The following papers were read : —

"Thomas Hancock, a Native of Lexington," by Rev. C. A. Staples.

"Captain John Parker," by Miss E. S. Parker.

APRIL 12, 1887.

Regular meeting. Vice-President H. G. Locke in the chair.

The following gifts were presented to the Society : —

An old muster roll, by Dr. R. M. Lawrence

Two muster rolls of the companies commanded by Captains William and Benjamin Reed, by Messrs. Charles M. and Theodore J. Parker.

An old tavern sign, with a portrait of John Hancock painted thereon, and a picture, by Miss Ellen A. Stone.

A pair of spectacles worn by Mrs. Mary Sanderson, and a pocket knife and mortar used by the same lady.

The following papers were presented: —

"The First Normal School in America," by Miss Rebecca D. Viles.

"Reminiscences of a Participant in the Events of April 19, 1775," by George O. Smith.

"The Pitcairn Family," by Rev. E. G. Porter.

CELEBRATION OF THE ONE HUNDRED AND TWELFTH ANNIVERSARY OF THE BATTLE OF LEXINGTON.

A general meeting of citizens was holden in the Town Hall on Sunday evening. The hall was filled to its utmost capacity. Music was furnished by a chorus under the direction of Professor H. E. Holt. Addresses were delivered by Rev. L. B. Hatch and E. H. Capen, D.D.

On the morning of the 19th, at an early hour, the First Regiment Drum and Fife Corps marched through the streets of the town, arousing the people by their patriotic music. An old-fashioned breakfast was served at the Massachusetts House. In the afternoon, an entertainment was given in the Town Hall, designed especially for the children. The music was under the direction of Mrs. H. E. Holt. Rev. C. A. Staples delivered an address descriptive of the appearance of the town and of the battle fought on the 19th of April, 1775. Addresses were also made by Rev. C. J. Staples, of Reading, and Rev. W. L. Robbins, of Lexington, and several selections were read by Miss Jessie Eldridge. In the evening, a social party was held in the Town Hall.

The hall was decorated with beautiful plants, and the music was furnished by Richardson's Orchestra.

OCTOBER 11, 1887.

Regular meeting. President Scott in the chair.

Dr. Seth Saltmarsh read a paper on "John Wyckliffe : His Influence on the Revolution."

Rev. G. W. Porter, D.D., presented to the Society the "Oration of General Joseph Warren, delivered March 6, 1775, on the Boston Massacre," and read a brief sketch of General Warren's life and extracts from the oration.

DECEMBER 13, 1887.

Regular meeting. President Scott in the chair.

The following gifts were presented to the Society: —

Copy of the *Independent Chronicle;* pair of shoe-buckles belonging to Elisha Whitney, great-grandfather of Mrs. J. Q. A. Chandler; picture of the hospital of Sir Robert Dudley; also a large collection of original deeds of various estates in Lexington, many containing the names of old families,—all from Mr. and Mrs. J. Q. A. Chandler.

An old paper containing an account of the coronation of Queen Victoria, by Miss Louisa Angier.

An autograph letter of Laura Bridgman, by Rev. Dr. Porter.

An old deed of Samuel Stone to David Fiske, dated 1664, probably conveying the present Cary farm, by William H. Smith.

Portrait of Jonathan Harrington, with autograph, by Mrs. Warren Duren.

The historian read a report referring to the important events connected with the town during the year, among which was the offer to the town by Hon. William A. Tower of a beautiful library building and of a site for the same by Miss Alice B. Cary.

The following papers were read: —

"John Hancock," by L. E. Bennink.

"The Old Taverns of Lexington," by E. P. Bliss.

"Modes of Conveyance through Lexington before the Railroads," by George O. Smith.

FEBRUARY 14, 1888.

Regular meeting. President Scott in the chair.

The following gifts to the Society were announced: —

A copy of the sermon of Rev. Avery Williams on the one hundredth anniversary of the incorporation of Lexington, from Miss Sarah Chandler.

A daguerreotype of Theodore Parker and a portrait of his study, from Miss Matilda Goodwin.

An inkstand used by Theodore Parker, from Mrs. Curtis, of Boston.

A piece of wood, a portion of the belfry of the old North Church, from which were swung the Paul Revere lanterns on the night of April 18, 1775, from Albert T. Whiting, of Boston.

Committees were appointed to take charge of the celebration of the 19th of April, and to secure an appropriation by the town for the purpose.

The following papers were read: —

"Early Parish and Town Government in Massachusetts," by Robert P. Clapp.

"Lexington Academy and its Building," by Hon. A. E. Scott.

APRIL 10, 1888.

Annual meeting. President Scott in the chair.

The annual reports of the officers were read and accepted.

The following officers were elected:

President, M. H. Merriam.

Vice-Presidents, Albert S. Parsons, Charles A. Wellington, Harry W. Davis, Mrs. C. C. Goodwin, Mrs. Theodore C. Robinson.

Corresponding Secretary, Dr. Robert M. Lawrence.

Recording Secretary and Clerk, L. E. Bennink.

Historian, Rev. C. A. Staples.

Custodian, Emory A. Mulliken.

Treasurer, L. A. Saville.

The president-elect was escorted to the chair, and made a brief speech of acceptance.

A letter from the Worcester Society of Antiquity was read, accepting an invitation to visit Lexington; and a committee of seven was appointed to arrange for their reception.

Rev. C. A. Staples read a paper entitled "The Story of the Hancock-Clark House in Lexington," giving its history, and citing many of the events and associations that make it memorable in our history, closing with an eloquent appeal for its preservation.

CELEBRATION OF THE ONE HUNDRED AND THIRTEENTH ANNIVERSARY OF THE BATTLE OF LEXINGTON.

Commemorative services were held in the Town Hall, Sunday evening, April 15. Appropriate music was furnished by a select chorus, under the direction of Professor Holt. An address was delivered by Mrs. Mary A. Livermore. Subject, "The Women of the Revolution."

At sunrise and sunset on Thursday, April 19, bells were rung; and at an early hour the Massachusetts First Regiment Drum Corps marched over the route taken by the British troops April 19, 1775.

An old-fashioned breakfast was served at the Massachusetts House, which was largely participated in by our citizens.

In the afternoon a large audience gathered in the Town Hall to listen to exercises arranged especially for the instruction and entertainment of the children of the public schools. Instrumental music was furnished by the band, and the children joined in singing patriotic songs. A recitation was given by Master Warren A. Lord, of Boston. An address was delivered by Colonel T. W. Higginson. Subject, "Opening Scenes of the Civil War"; and short addresses were given by others. The celebration closed with a grand promenade concert and ball at the Town Hall in the evening.

VISIT OF THE WORCESTER SOCIETY OF ANTIQUITY TO LEXINGTON, JUNE 16, 1888.

The Worcester Society of Antiquity are accustomed to have an annual Field Day in Summer, on which they visit some historic town and spend the day in making themselves familiar with the locality, and the interesting events associated with it. Knowing this fact, the Lexington Historical Society extended an invitation to them to make Lexington the place of their Field Day, and to accept its hospitality on that occasion. The invitation, voted at the meeting in March, 1888, was gratefully accepted; and subsequently a committee of ladies and gentlemen was appointed by the Lexington Society to make all necessary arrangements for their entertainment. Saturday, June 16, was the day chosen for the excursion; and upwards of eighty persons came in the company. They were received by the Lexington committee on their arrival at the station, and conducted to the Town Hall, where an address of welcome was made by President M. H. Merriam and responded to by Mr. E. B. Crane of the Worcester Society. Rev. C. A. Staples then gave some account of the events which have made Lexington renowned in the history of our country and the spots identified with them. The party then proceeded to visit the Common, and the houses around it marked with memorial tablets, and the monument to Captain John Parker in the old cemetery, ending with a collation in the vestry of the Unitarian church, prepared by the committee, which was duly appreciated by the guests. In the afternoon, carriages were taken from the church, and a visit made to the splendid rhododendron exhibition of Mrs. Francis B. Hayes, with a drive through her beautiful grounds, calling on the way at the Hancock-Clark House, which proved to be an object of great interest to the visitors, and was kindly opened to their inspection by the occupants. Afterwards a visit was made to the old Munroe Tavern, which was generously opened by the proprietor, who also dispensed something of the kindly cheer for which it was famous in the olden time. Finally, the company assembled in the hall of Cary Library, where, after an examination of the many interesting and precious relics of antiquity which it contains, resolutions were passed by the guests, thanking the Lexington Historical Society for their generous hospitality and for the interesting and profitable day they had enjoyed. Thus ended an occasion of mutual acquaintance and fellowship by two societies engaged in a common object, which is remembered with pleasure by all.

OCTOBER 9, 1888.

Regular meeting. Vice-President Parsons in the chair.

The historian made a brief report touching recent events. The corresponding secretary presented data regarding Fort Castle William, now known as Fort Independence, in Boston Harbor. He also presented to the Society the "History of North America," by Rev. Mr. Cooper.

A paper was read by Rev. C. A. Staples, entitled, "Were the Old Times Better than the New in Lexington?"

DECEMBER 11, 1888.

Owing to a violent storm, no meeting was held.

FEBRUARY 12, 1889.

Regular meeting. President Merriam in the chair.

Committees were appointed to arrange for the celebration of the 19th of April and to obtain an appropriation from the town therefor.

Rev. G. W. Porter, D.D., loaned the Society the commission of Major Moses Porter, signed by John Adams, President of the United States, and Samuel Dexter, Secretary of War. A paper was read by Rev. Alfred P. Putnam, D.D., of Concord, Mass., entitled "General Moses Porter, an Unrecognized Hero of American History."

PROCEEDINGS.

MARCH 12, 1889.

Annual meeting. President Merriam in the chair.
The following officers were elected: —
President, M. H. Merriam.
Vice-Presidents, F. O. Vaille, George O. Smith, George C. Goodwin, Miss F. M. Robinson, Miss Clara Harrington.
Historian, Rev. C. A. Staples.
Custodian, Emory A. Mulliken.
Recording Secretary, L. E. Benniuk.
Corresponding Secretary, Albert S. Parsons.
Treasurer, L. A. Saville.

A committee was appointed to secure, if possible, for the Society the Diary of Rev. Jonas Clark.

The Council was instructed to arrange for the proper celebration of the one hundredth anniversary of the visit of President Washington to Lexington, Nov. 5, 1789.

A cannon-ball recently dug up in the meadow north of the battle-ground, supposed to have been fired April 19, 1775, was presented by Miss F. M. Robinson.

The following papers were read: —
"1775 and 1861," by G. W. Sampson.
"An Account of the First Proprietors of Lexington Village," by Rev. C. A. Staples.

APRIL 9, 1889.

Regular meeting. President Merriam in the chair.

Rev C. A. Staples, Rev. E. G. Porter, and Mrs. Rebecca E. Robinson were appointed a committee to arrange the proceedings of the Society for publication.

The historian gave a detailed account of the visit of the Worcester Society of Antiquity to Lexington. He also called attention to the loose manner of preserving the old records of Lexington. A committee was appointed to arrange with the Worcester Society of Antiquity for a joint meeting on the old Indian battle-ground at Sudbury.

The following papers were read: —
"Charles Hudson," by W. W. Spencer.
"The Shelter, Clothing, and Subsistence of the Olden Time," by M. H. Merriam.

CELEBRATION OF THE ONE HUNDRED AND FOURTEENTH ANNIVERSARY OF THE BATTLE OF LEXINGTON.

Rev. Minot J. Savage, of Boston, delivered an address to a large audience in the Town Hall, on Sunday evening, April 14. Subject, "General Washington."

Friday, April 19, was observed in substantially the same manner as in previous years. A pleasant feature of the day was the display of national colors throughout the town.

Rev. Edward Everett Hale delivered the address at the children's ntertainment in the afternoon, descriptive of the ride of Paul Revere, the march of Lord Percy, and the subsequent events on Lexington Green, closing with an original poem entitled "New England Chevy Chace."

The Massachusetts Sixth Regiment Association visited Lexington during the day, and were escorted by George G. Meade, Post 119, G. A. R., to the battle-ground.

OCTOBER 8, 1889.

Regular meeting. President Merriam in the chair.

The following books were presented to the Society by William Power Wilson, of Boston : —

One volume Colonial Laws from 1670 to 1672.
One volume Colonial Laws from 1672 to 1685.
Old State House Memorial.
Sheridan Memorial.
Paine Burgess Memorial.

Engravings of William Lloyd Garrison and Wendell Phillips, and a photograph of the Parker Monument, were presented from Mrs. Sarah Otis, of Boston.

The clerk reported for the Council the programme arranged for the observance of the anniversary of Washington's visit to Lexington.

Rev. C. A. Staples, for the Committee on Publications, reported that they had arranged for publication, with the proceedings, fourteen of the papers which had been read before the Society since its organization,—by vote of the Society, the committee were confined to those papers which related to our local history, and thus others equally worthy of publication were excluded ; that the Society was indebted to Mrs. Frances C. Babcock and Mr. Charles A. Wellington for their assistance in reproducing the first school-house erected in Lexington, and the second and third meeting-houses, together with the interior of the second meeting-house, showing the arrangement of the pews.

A committee was appointed to consider the expediency of adopting some plan by which the old town records may be more safely kept and arranged for the use of those who are interested in historical matters.

Rev. C. A. Staples read a paper entitled "The Villages of the Praying Indians in the Massachusetts Colony."

Nov. 5, 1889.

The one hundredth anniversary of Washington's visit to Lexington was observed by the Historical Society with appropriate services on Tuesday, Nov. 5, 1889.

The Council was instructed by vote of the Society at the regular meeting on Tuesday evening, April 9, to adopt such measures for a due observance of the occasion as they should deem advisable. Accordingly, different committees were appointed to take charge of the proceedings and carry out the instructions of the Council.

The plan adopted was to visit the old Munroe tavern where Washington dined on Tuesday afternoon, and inspect the relics gathered there connected with him and with events of our town history, ending with a banquet at the Russell House at 6 P. M. This plan proved to be a satisfactory one, and was well executed by the various committees. During the afternoon a large number of people, including many of the pupils in the public schools, visited the Munroe tavern, where they were kindly received by the proprietor, Mr. William Munroe, and by the occupants, Mr. and Mrs. Champney, and shown through the different rooms of this interesting old house. The collection of relics loaned by various persons for the occasion, a list of which will be found printed at end of Proceedings, was large and valuable, and called forth many expressions of interest and delight. In the evening at the appointed hour, the members of the Society with their friends and invited guests assembled at the Russell House, where a bountiful collation was spread in the large hall, which had been handsomely decorated with flowers for the occasion. Among the decorations was a large and elegant flower piece, designed and presented by Mr. Frank B. Hayes, composed of chrysanthemums, pinks, and azaleas, bordered with delicate ferns, and bearing across the face the name "Washington" in blue violets, and below the dates 1789-1889.

PROCEEDINGS.

The divine blessing was invoked by Rev. G. W. Porter, D.D.; and, after a full discussion of the viands with which the tables were spread, the president, Mr. Matthew H. Merriam, called the assembly to order, and opened the literary entertainment with the following address of welcome:—

ADDRESS OF THE PRESIDENT.

Members of the Lexington Historical Society:

Ladies and Gentlemen,—It gives me pleasure to welcome you one and all to this festival to-night, in commemoration of an event full of interest to the people of this town. We are here, not only as students of history, concerned in the verification of its facts and their relations, but to draw from them, as we contemplate the life, character, and influence of the most eminent personage in American history, inspirations which shall kindle in our breasts anew sentiments of lofty patriotism, of disinterested devotion to the common welfare, the purification and elevation of sound politics, as exemplified by the grand qualities of mind and heart of Washington.

It is opportune that the day we celebrate occurs on this election day, in which we have been permitted to exercise the high privilege and duty of American citizenship, for which we are indebted more than to any other to the sturdy probity, patriotic purposes, indomitable courage, persistent patience, amid the most trying circumstances in the darkest periods of our history, to that prophet whose far-seeing intelligence presaged a government founded on the will of the people.

His tour in the fall of 1789 in these Northern States had a greater significance and political importance than has been customary to accord to it, if we may judge by the scant place it has had in the memoirs of his life. To appreciate this, we need to recall the political condition of the colonies for the ten years previous, embracing the period of Washington's more prominent participation in colonial affairs.

There was the breaking away from the ties of fatherland and an established government, and entering upon that period of uncertainties which followed, compelled to carry on a long and tedious warfare for self-preservation, supported with grudging assistance from separate and diversely interested colonies, torn by divisions, jealousies, and rival ambitions, and weighted down by the incubus of an imbecile Continental Congress, having the show and pretence of a government, without ability to enforce its decrees or raise a dollar in money; these culminating in the framing in convention of that *new* device, the Federal Constitution.

When that Constitution was launched and committed to its fate, it was by no means the popular measure we may suppose it to have been: it was regarded with doubt and misgivings, assailed with violent opposition. In Massachusetts even, it was hesitatingly adopted by a small majority. Yet in all this turmoil and distraction we behold the towering genius of Washington prevailing over all by the tremendous force of his personality. With wonderful insight, more than others, he saw the glorious possibilities of the future; and to the accomplishment of these he directed all the energies of his versatile powers.

When that Constitution was finally adopted, and Washington unanimously selected as the first President, he felt keenly the responsibilities of the administration of it, and had great anxiety for its ultimate success. The majority was too narrow to be trusted for permanent results. He was not deceived by his personal popularity, but knew as well as anybody that a large element of it was due to the attachment to his person by the army. A very different thing this from an obedience to the cold forms of stable laws, a passive, not to say active or enthusiastic, support of new, untried, and questionable forms of government.

From New York, south, his contact with the leading men of the time and his indefatigable persistence secured large support for the new government. Massachusetts, New Hampshire, and Connecticut needed harmonizing and consolidation in support of it. Hence the significance and importance of meeting the people of these States, in order to fortify and confirm the loyalty of the people. The power of his commanding presence, the magnetism of his person, the gravity of his speech, swayed men, and his *dictum* ended controversy and compacted union. The tidal wave of enthusiasm swept away opposition, and the new government settled to its firm foundations. Such were some of the effects of that memorial visit to these States. As he passed through these streets in profound sympathy with the brave men who fought on yonder green, he donned his military uniform, and thus identified himself with those heroes of the Revolution and did special honor to our town.

From that time till now, Lexington and Massachusetts have never swerved from true loyalty and devoted patriotism.

Ladies and gentlemen, let the genius of Washington be our guest to-night; let us light afresh the torch of liberty with a purer flame, and pass the fire to posterity through ages yet to come,

> "Till old time shall hide the sun in gloom,
> And this proud empire seeks its laureled tomb."

Song by a quartet choir led by Prof. H. E. Holt, "Hail Columbia."

The president then introduced Rev. C. A. Staples as follows: Among the remarkable things that Washington did is that he kept a diary. I take it that a man who can keep a diary continuously and persistently has in him some element of greatness. Washington was pre-eminently a silent man, but in his diary which he faithfully kept we learn much of the man himself that we can find out from no other sources. One of our number has given that diary careful attention, and we shall be pleased to hear from his gleanings in that direction that our knowledge of the character of Washington may be more complete.

I have the pleasure to introduce to you the Rev. C. A. Staples, of Lexington.

WASHINGTON'S VISIT TO LEXINGTON

Nov. 5, 1789.

WASHINGTON visited New England at four different times. First, in the year after General Braddock's defeat, February, 1756, he came to Boston to consult with Governor Shirley, Commander-in-Chief of his Majesty's forces in North America, in regard to the precedence of rank between British and colonial officers. At this time, he was in command of the Virginia militia. He wished to know whether precedence of rank was to be determined by seniority of commission, as he contended it should be, or by the service to which one belonged. The British officers maintained that they outranked the American or colonial officers, because they were in the service of the king. Washington gained his point; and the vexed question, which had caused much bickering and bitterness, was ended. He was then twenty-four years old, and not unlikely he had another object in view besides the settling of military rank in his first visit to New England. In coming here and returning, at that time, he stopped at the house of Beverley Robinson in New York, where the beautiful Mary Phillipse was staying, and, it is said, urged what proved an unsuccessful suit for her hand. His second visit was nineteen years afterward, — namely, in July, 1775, — when he came to take command of the American troops around Boston and assume the military leadership of the patriotic cause. Here he remained conducting the siege of Boston until March of the following year, when the British were driven out of the town by the ever-tightening cords which he drew around it. The third visit, that which we have met to commemorate, took place in 1789, six months after his inauguration as President of the United States. It was undertaken, as he says, to see how the people were affected toward the new government, and to learn the actual condition of the country, its agriculture, manufactures, and commerce. His retinue consisted of his two secretaries, Dr. Tobias Lear and Major Jackson, and six servants, probably negro slaves. He rode in his own carriage drawn by four horses, — "driven in hand," probably the postilion and footman on the outside, Washington with his secretaries inside, and four servants on their horses in advance. Thus the party consisted of nine men and eight horses, with the heavy cumbersome but stylish English carriage. We can well imagine what a sensation the arrival and departure of so striking a procession must have caused in the quiet villages through which it passed. The people were unused to such splendid equipages as that of the President. Even stage-coaches were then rare in New England. Washington took great pride in fine horses, elegant carriages, and substantial trappings and equipments of every sort. He always ordered the best of materials in clothing and furniture for himself and family. He liked to see richly dressed ladies at his receptions, and often notes the number of such in his diary. He had the stately manners of an English gentleman of the eighteenth century, and strictly observed the etiquette which he thought becoming his station, and expected it of those who visited him. The plain, Puritanic New England people, accustomed to a state of society where almost universal equality prevailed, were much impressed by the dignity and splendor of Washington's party. They had seldom or never seen such a display of fine horses and servants. Even Governor Hancock, travelling in his dashing red coach drawn by four horses, with postilion and footman mounted [in their places, did not rival the impressive dignity of the President in his great carriage rolling slowly on from town to town.

Washington's plan of the journey was carefully formed before starting. He fixed upon his route, the time he would give to it, the stopping places, and the objects to be noticed; and he was reluctant to deviate from his plan in the slightest particular. He aimed to travel from thirty to forty miles each day, starting early in the morning, and going ten or fifteen miles, then stopping for an hour or two to breakfast and to feed the horses, afterward resuming the journey and continuing until dinner time, then another rest and meal, and after that travelling on until he had reached the tavern where he was to spend the night. He did not accept of private hospitality, except to dine or sup with some public man, but always went to houses of public entertainment, where he could pay his own bills. He intended to avoid military receptions and parades, and discouraged them whenever informed of their preparation; but he could not prevent the assembling of the militia and firing of salutes in the principal towns on his arrival and departure, nor the addresses of civic, religious, and educational bodies in the towns through which he passed. No doubt these often gave him much annoyance; but he received them courteously, and invariably replied — either at the time they were given in a formal speech or afterwards in writing.

Starting from New York on Thursday, Oct. 15, 1789, about nine o'clock, he proceeds slowly over the rough roads along the shore of the Sound, arriving at Fairfield in Connecticut after two days' journeying. In his diary, noting the events and observations of each day, are many interesting and curious facts. Thus he records that the cattle are of good quality, and that every farm-house abounds in geese, the roads are extremely rough and the land stony, but covered with grass and good crops of Indian corn. The hogs are large, but rather long legged. No house is seen without a chimney of stone or brick, and rarely without a shingled roof, and generally the sides are shingled. The country is immensely stony. At Fairfield, he tells us that the superb landscape to be seen from the meeting-house is a rich regalia. The farmers are busy in gathering their apples and making cider, the apple crop rather above mediocrity. The average yield of wheat about fifteen bushels to the acre, but often twenty to twenty-five. Destructive vidences of British cruelty during the war are yet visible. The chimneys of many burnt houses are standing. The principal exports are horses and cattle, salted beef and pork; lumber and corn to the West Indies, and in a small degree wheat and flour.

He leaves Fairfield a little after sunrise, and rides ten miles to Stamford to breakfast. "Here I was received with an effort of military parade, and attended to the ferry, which is near half a mile wide. At Milford, I saw the handsome cascade over the tumbling dam. One of the prettiest things of this kind, however, is at Stamford. It is near a hundred yards wide, and the water now being of a proper height and the rays of the sun falling upon it as we passed had a pretty effect upon the foaming water as it fell." He reaches New Haven on Saturday afternoon, having missed on the road a committee of the legislature sent out to receive him, but did not escape their address, and also one from the clergy the same evening, and a visit from the governor, lieutenant-governor, and mayor. At New Haven, he remains over Sunday, attending the Episcopal church in the morning and the Congregational in the afternoon. The State officials dined with him at the house of Mr. Brown "who keeps a good tavern."

"In the evening received the officers of the State belonging to the late Continental Army, and drank tea with the mayor, Roger Sherman." Then followed statistics of the population, the churches, Yale College, the exports, the tonnage on the river, and the depth of water,—everything, in short, relating to the trade and growth of the town. Monday, at six o'clock, he is again on the way riding thirteen miles to breakfast and reaching Hartford at three in the afternoon. Here he remains during the following day, Tuesday visiting a woollen factory where broadcloth was made, and ordering a suit sent him at New York and "a whole piece of Everlasting to make breeches for my servant." Then we have the usual accounts of trade, commerce, population, and the depth of the river. The next afternoon at four, he arrives in Springfield, examines the continental stores, which he found in good condition, especially the powder, which he says "was very dry; but the barracks and the laboratory belonging to the United States are in a decaying state." He stops at Parson's tavern in Springfield which he pronounces as a good house, where he was visited by the adjutant-general of Massachusetts and other military and civic officials. He remarks that "there is a great equality in the people of Connecticut, few or no opulent men and no poor,

great similitude in their buildings, the general fashion of which is
a chimney (always of stone or brick) and door in the middle,
with a staircase fronting the door and running up by the side of
the chimney, two flush stories, with a very good show of sash and
glass windows. The size is generally from thirty to fifty feet in
length and from twenty to thirty in width, exclusive of a back
shed, which seems to be added as the family increases. The farms
are small, not averaging more than one hundred acres; and they
are worked chiefly by oxen, which have no other feed than hay,
with a horse and sometimes two before them, both in plough and
cart. In their light lands and in their sleighs, they work horses,
but find them much more expensive. Springfield stands under the
hill on interval land, and has but one meeting-house. On Thursday, set out at seven o'clock, and rode over an almost uninhabited
pine plain for eight miles, and then, before the road descends into
the valley of the Chicopee, it is hilly, rocky and steep, and continues so for many miles, till we came to Palmer, where we breakfasted at the house of one Scott. Among these pines are ponds of
fresh water. From Palmer to Brookfield to one Hitchcock's, fifteen
miles farther, part of which is pretty good and part over the hills
is very bad; but, when over, the ground begins to get tolerably
good and the country better cultivated, though crops of corn do
not look well, and have been injured, it is said, by an early frost in
September. A beautiful fresh-water pond and large is in the plain
at Brookfield. The fashion of the houses is more diversified than
in Connecticut, though many are built in their style. The enclosures have but indifferent fences, wood or stone, according as the
country abounds in the latter, of which it is full after passing the
pine levels. At Brookfield fed the horses and despatched an express sent by Governor Hancock, giving notice of the measures he
was about to pursue for my reception on the road and in Boston,
with a request to lodge at his house [which he respectfully declines]. Continued on to Spencer, through pretty good roads, ten
miles, and lodged at the house of one Jenks, who keeps a pretty
good tavern. Friday, commenced our course with the sun, and,
passing through Leicester, met some gentlemen of the town of
Worcester, to escort us on our way. Arrived at ten o'clock and
breakfasted. Here we were received by a handsome company of
militia artillery in uniform, who saluted with thirteen guns on our
entry and departure. At this place also, we met a committee of

the town of Boston and an adjutant of Major-General Brooks, of the Middlesex militia, who had proceeded to this place in order to make some arrangements of military and other parade on my way to and in the town of Boston, and to fix with me on the hours at which I should pass through Cambridge and enter Boston. Finding that this ceremony was not to be avoided, though I had made every effort to do it, I named the hour of ten to pass the militia of Middlesex Country at Cambridge and the hour of twelve to enter Boston. On the line between Worcester and Middlesex, I was met by a troop of light horse, who escorted me to Marlborough, sixteen miles, where we dined, and thence to Weston, where we lodged. The country about Worcester, and onwards toward Boston is better improved and the lands of better quality than we travelled through yesterday. The crops, it is said, have been good. Indian corn, rye, buckwheat, and grass, with beef, pork and cattle, are the produce of the farms. Saturday, 24th, dressed by seven o'clock and set out by eight. At ten arrived in Cambridge, according to appointment, but the militia were not in line until eleven. They made, however, an excellent appearance, with General Brooks at their head. At this place the lieutenant governor, Mr. Samuel Adams, with the executive council, met me, and preceded my entrance into town, which was in every degree flattering and honorable."

I will now leave the transcript of the diary, and give a brief narrative of the subsequent proceedings. Washington had already been detained an hour longer at Cambridge than he expected, waiting for the militia; and, when he arrived at the line between Roxbury and Boston, another long delay occurred. Here the selectmen of Boston claimed him as the guest of the town; but the State authorities had already assumed the care of the presidential party, and insisted upon retaining it. The day was wet and cold; and Washington became impatient over the miserable bickering, and at last called upon his aide to show him some other way into the town by which he could be rid of this wrangling. Finally, the State authorities yielded precedence to the selectmen; and the procession passed down what is now Washington Street to the old State House, where a splendid arch had been thrown over the street, with a canopy above it twenty feet in height, on which an American eagle perched. He entered the State House by the south door, and came out upon the balcony fronting Washington Street, where an immense concourse of people, filling the streets and the windows and covering the roofs of the buildings, greeted him with an enthusiastic welcome. Then followed an ode, he says, "addressed to the President, and well sung by a band of select singers, followed by a procession of the trades and mechanics of the town." He soon retired to his lodgings at Widow Ingersoll's which, he says, is a very decent and good house. This was at the corner of Tremont and Court Streets, where the new Hemingway Building now stands. Washington had engaged to dine at Governor Hancock's on this day; but the governor had not come to meet him, and he decided to break the engagement, dining at his lodgings with the Vice-President, John Adams, "who," he says, "favored me with his company." This was a great disappointment and mortification to Hancock, who had set his heart upon entertaining the President in his splendid mansion, and prepared a sumptuous dinner for the occasion. But Washington believed that Governor Hancock did not come out to receive and welcome him because he held himself to be superior to the President in the State of Massachusetts, where he was the head of the government. This he would not concede. Massachusetts was only a part of the nation, and the authority of the nation was supreme over all its parts. He represented that authority, and it must be acknowledged supreme in every part of the country. "I shall not see Governor Hancock," he said to Samuel Adams and the council, "unless at my own lodgings. This," he says, "I told them in explicit terms." Washington was no stickler for personal honors, but he was no believer in the doctrine of State rights. We were now one nation, and not thirteen independent nations; and he meant that fact should be recognized in every quarter of the Union. This occurred on Saturday night. Sunday he attended worship at King's Chapel, the Episcopal church, in the morning, and at Brattle Street Congregational in the afternoon. In the mean time, Governor Hancock had seen the folly of trying to set himself above the President, even in Boston. The people were indignant at his conduct, and he was compelled to yield. Accordingly, he wrote to Washington, saying: "If agreeable to your Excellency, I will call upon you at some hour this afternoon. I am suffering extremely from an attack of the gout, and it may be at the peril of my life. But I am resolved to do myself the honor, if it be agreeable to the President." Washington replied that it would give him great pleasure to receive a visit from Governor Hancock at any hour, but begged him not to endanger his life by such an exposure; that it gave him great pain to hear of the governor's illness, and he trusted that he might speedily recover. At the appointed time the governor came, swathed in flannel, and borne in the arms of his servants, to Washington's lodgings, where in his person Massachusetts paid due obeisance to the supremacy of the nation, — an obeisance which she has cheerfully paid from that day to this.

On Monday, it was cold and rainy; and Washington was suffering from a cold caught while waiting at Cambridge and during the exposure of his reception in Boston. One eye was badly inflamed, and he felt obliged to give up his proposed visit to Lexington on that day. It had been a part of his plan to make a special visit to this town, where, he says, "the first blood in the dispute with Great Britain was drawn." Probably, had this plan been carried out, he would have received a formal reception here; but he was obliged to defer his visit to a later and an uncertain date, which accounts for the fact that no preparation was made here to give him a public reception. But, in spite of the cold and the inflamed eye, he drank tea with Governor Hancock on Monday evening, when doubtless a complete reconciliation took place over the fragrant beverage in the governor's beautiful china, of which he was very proud. On the following day, Tuesday, Washington was again on the move, first receiving the clergy of the town, and afterwards, at eleven in the forenoon, attending an oratorio at King's Chapel. Then followed addresses from the governor and council, from the selectmen of Boston, and from the president of Harvard College; and at three in the afternoon he partook of an elegant dinner at Faneuil Hall, given by the State authorities. These long ceremonies seem to have cured the cold and the inflamed eye; and the next day he was ready for wider explorations, visiting the manufacturing establishments and the forts and gun-ships in the harbor, and, as usual, noting statistics of various kinds, dining at Mr. Bowdoin's and attending an assembly in the evening, where, he says, "were one hundred ladies, whose appearance was elegant, and many of them very handsome."

His stay in Boston was now ended; and on Thursday morning he goes out to Cambridge through Charlestown, but, strangely enough, does not mention Bunker Hill, which he must have passed on the way, and where the famous redoubt thrown up by the Americans was then plainly seen. President Willard shows him the orrery, the library of thirteen thousand volumes, and the museum of Harvard, after which he proceeds on his way through Lynn to Marblehead, which he much desired to see, and thence to Salem, where he passed the night, attending an assembly in the evening. Here, again, he meets "one hundred handsome, well-dressed ladies," but does not fail to notice the cotton manufacturing and the commerce. On Saturday he reaches Portsmouth, and is welcomed by the citizens with odes sung to his honor and speeches made in his praise. Sunday he goes to the Episcopal church in the morning and to the Congregational in the afternoon, Dr. Buckminster's. Then followed two days of sight seeing, visiting the harbor, fort, and light-house, taking a fishing excursion, and, as he says, catching two or three cod; but he modestly refrains from telling how much they weighed, — a worthy example to all amateur fishermen. The fatigue of the day's sport, however, caused him to retire at seven o'clock. But he did not escape the inevitable addresses from church and State authorities, nor the evening assembly, where "seventy-five well-dressed and handsome ladies appeared," among whom he says, "was a greater proportion with much blacker hair than is usually seen in the Southern States." In Portsmouth, he was requested to sit for his portrait, and kindly consented, giving up two hours to that delightful occupation.

And now, having reached the limit of his proposed tour, he turns his face homeward. On Wednesday morning, November 4, he leaves Portsmouth for Exeter, and pushes on to Haverhill, where he passes the night. At sunrise on the morning of the 5th, one hundred years ago to-day, he leaves for Andover, breakfasting at Abbott's tavern in that town, where he met with much attention from Mr. Samuel Phillips. "Mr. Phillips accompanied me through Billariki to Lexington, where I dined, and viewed the spot on which the first blood was spilt on the 19th April, 1775. Here I parted with Mr. Phillips, and proceeded to Watertown, 8 miles. We lodged at the house of a Widow Coolidge near the bridge, and a very indifferent house it is." He speaks of the country between Lexington and Watertown as very pleasant, and the roads as generally good, but expresses some indignation that he should have been directed to go through Watertown instead of Waltham, thereby adding five miles to the length of his journey, which he would gladly have been spared, and the night at Widow Coolidge's "very indifferent house." But the widow did not keep him long in the morning. He was up and off at an early hour, riding sixteen miles before breakfast, which he took at Sherborn; and in the evening of that day he reached Taft's tavern in the western part of Uxbridge, where he passed the night. The quaint old house is still standing, and remains in almost precisely the same condition it was when Washington was its guest, and is still owned and occupied by the Tafts. Washington had purposed to pass the night at Mendon, five miles this side, at the tavern of Colonel Amidown; but he found the proprietor absent, and his wife too sick or too scared to receive them, and so he passed on to Uxbridge, where the Mendon people went to call upon him in the evening. He had already retired when they arrived, and they were keenly disappointed; but, being informed of the matter, he rose, dressed himself, and received them in the kindest manner, though the ladies were not probably so handsome or so richly dressed as those whom he had received in Boston, Salem, and Portsmouth. But they had come many miles on horseback that chilly November evening to pay their respects to the President, and he said, "They shall not be disappointed." At this old tavern of Taft's were two young girls, the landlord's daughters, one of whom was named for Mrs. Washington, Martha W. Taft.

He had never heard of them before. They were bright, modest girls, and showed much attention to Washington, trying to make him as comfortable as possible in what must have been even then a rather forlorn place. On reaching Hartford the following Monday, November 9, he wrote their father this letter, namely: —

"*Sir*, — Being informed that you have given my name to one of your sons and called another after Mrs. Washington's family, and being, moreover, very much pleased with the modest and innocent looks of your two daughters, Patty and Polly, I do for these reasons send each of these girls a piece of chintz; and to Patty, who bears the name of Mrs. Washington, and who waited upon us more than Polly did, I send five guineas, with which she may buy herself any little ornaments she may want, or she may dispose of them in any other manner more agreeable to herself.

"As I do not give these things with a view to have it talked of, or even to its being known, the less there is said about the matter, the better you will please me; but that I may be sure that the chintz and money have got safe to hand, let Patty, who I dare say is equal to it, write me a line informing me thereof, directed to the President of the United States at New York. I wish you and your family well, and am your humble servant,

"GEORGE WASHINGTON."

On the following day, Saturday, November 7, he left Taft's at sunrise with the purpose of visiting General Putnam at Pomfret; but, finding that it would be five miles out of his way, and that it would considerably delay his journey and derange his plans, he gave it up, and went on to Ashford, Conn., where he lodged at the tavern of Squire Perkins and spent the Sabbath. I copy the entry in the diary for Sunday entire. It is as follows: "*Sunday, 8th.* — It being contrary to law and disagreeable to the people of this State to travel on the Sabbath day, and my horses, after passing through such intolerable roads, wanting rest, I stayed at Perkin's tavern (which, by the bye, is not a good one) all day ; and, a meeting-house being within a few rods of the door, I attended morning and evening service, and heard very lame discourses from a Mr. Pond."

Washington returned by nearly the same route through Connecticut that he came, reaching his house in New York at 3 P.M. on Friday, November 13, after an absence of about a month. It had been a long and tedious journey, over what he calls "amazingly crooked roads, made to suit the convenience of every man's fields, and the directions you receive from the people equally blind and ignorant."

In this diary of his journey, we are impressed with Washington's acuteness of observation, both in regard to things in general — the appearance of the country, the manners and characteristics of the people, their various industries and the sources of their prosperity — and also in regard to the minutest particulars of their thrift and welfare. He describes their crops, their houses, their cattle, fences rivers and forests. He saw everything with an understanding mind, and was wonderfully accurate and discriminating in his observations. Then, again, he impresses us as a man of inflexible will and indomitable energy. Nothing could turn him aside from his deliberate purpose and plan. It must be carried through. No amount of trouble and travel, of sight-seeing and speech hearing, of dinners and receptions, seemed to exhaust him. A rigid adherence to system, punctuality to the minute on every occasion, paying the last cent wherever due, and the same charges for his servants as for himself at the taverns, accepting no favors that he could not return, thoughtful, kind, and generous toward those who were associated with him and who served him, — such was the man whose visit to our historic town we celebrate to-night, as he appears in the brief records of his diary. In honoring the memory of one so just, so pure, so unselfish in his patriotism, so devoted to the interest and the service of the people, we are honoring that which is most sure of the everlasting remembrance of mankind.

President Merriam introduced the next speaker in the following words: —

On his way through our town, happily for us, and this day's celebration, Washington dined at the old Munroe tavern, which has been opened to us to-day that we might inspect the locality and see the things which he saw and handle the things which he handled. Most of us, I hope all, have made this pilgrimage to-day; and, as we reverently touched the things which the great man handled, it vividly brought to our minds the past and linked it with the present.

It is pleasant to remember that the descendants of Washington's host are still with us and still retain possession of the old hostelry. One of them will doubtless draw inspiration from these facts, having grown from childhood to manhood under the shadow of the old mansion and its wide-spreading elms. He is well fitted to give us an account of that dinner and the memorial associations connected therewith. I introduce to you Mr. James P. Munroe of Lexington.

WASHINGTON'S DINNER AT THE MUNROE TAVERN.

Ladies and Gentlemen, — When I was asked to assume the honorable task of representing my great-grandfather here to-night, I, naturally, searched the old Munroe tavern for memorials of him, but without success. A hunt through the garret of the old Mason house, was, however, more fortunate, as it resulted in this letter. The original, of which this is a copy, bears the date Nov. 7, 1789, and is indorsed, in a fine Italian hand, "Miss Sarah Munroe, Lexington, to Miss Mary Mason, New York." Sarah was the second daughter of Colonel William Munroe, the other children being William, Anna, Jonas, Lucinda, and Edmund. Mary was the only daughter of Mr. Joseph Mason, a famous pedagogue, and for many years, including 1789, town clerk. Of the reason of Miss Mason's sojourn in New York, we are not informed.

The letter is as follows: —

My ever deare Mary : —

I crave your patience in this Episle, as I must finish it to go by the Sunday Coach, and therfore indight it by a bad candle, dip'd, I warrant, by Brother Jonas, who is ever slack in all except his play. We have had great doings here. Our Loved President has journied here to Lex. & has took dinner at our very House. I suppose *you*, in the Great City of New York can have little interrest in the small haps of a Country Town, but *remember* it is the birth-place of you, and of American Freedom! I suppose, by this time, the Boston news have reached you, with the relation of the Jurney of Mr. Washington to Boston and of his reseption therein, how he stood many hours in the peircing Wind, waiting for an end to the bikkerings of the Honourable Selectmen, and how, therby, he incured a most vile *Grippe* wh. his loyal subjects thereupon took to themselves, being only too Happy, so they declared, to share even the Infloowenza with the Noble Washington! But know you, what the News-letters have doubtles not recount'd that this very infloowenza has been to my Respected Step-mother the cause of much Distres. For you must know that our reverend Parson having gone to Town of a friday, to see the great President and to aske the helth of his Cous[n] the Wurshipfull Gov. Hancock, w[ch] is sorely plaged with the Gowt, comes back with the tydings that M[r]. Washington with Gen[l]. Lincoln and many others with him, was Minded to come to Lexington of the Monday folowing, being the 26th of the last mo. And therupon did the Parson make, on the Sabbath, 3 most eddyfying Discourses, tending to prepare our Hearts for the Visit, (they being, of course, Decent, and touching upon Worldly things only so far as might be seemly.) Now, after 2d meeting, my respected Step-mother had much ado wether or no she could put the Pyes and pudings w[ch] we, with the aid of Mistress Downing and your Worthy Mother, had prepar'd on the Saturday, into the Oven on a Sabbath afternoon afore the Sun setting. Hapily the afternoon was over-cast and the hour of Setting come early. Then did we all, exsept the Children who have little care in these maters but to require to be constant Chid, set up the whole night to watch the oven lest some misschance befal the contents. You may juge we looked befrowzeled, come Morning, but soon after cork-Crow came a messenjer rid out at the Command of the Sec'y of the wurshipfull Gov[or], to tell us that M[r]. Washington was to sick, the infloowenza having seezed his left Eye, to attend us, the day being Raw and blusterry. Then such a borling as was heard from the children, espesialy Lucindy, who is ever forward in the making of noyse, and my step-Mother was like to say hard words dispite the Parson his so recent eddyfying Discourses. Now was great Questioning if his Highness (for so I like to call him) w^d come to our Town at all, till at last 'was roomered that having great Desire to see the field of Lexington, therefore he w^d turn his road in this Direction on his coming back from the State of New Hampshire. Mother, thereupon, bad Lucindy, who still borled lustyly, to make her respecs to naybors Mulliken and Downing (and I warrant you Naybors Mason were not forgot) and to ask them come eat the President his Feast. They all came in good time and my honnered Father set out to make them Merry, but it was easy seen that he tho't naybor Downing but a sorry makeshift for his exspected guest. *Your* good parrents be, of course, *always* Wellcome.

But you must be uneasy to hear tell of Mr. Washington his *real* Visit. 'Twas on Thursday last, and Wednesday, you may be bound, was a bussy day, what with Baking and mixing and the Brewwing of a fresh Lot of beer for the Flip. Then to, had all the plate to be scowr'd and the brases rubbed and the Floors new sanded ('tis a shame to my thinking, that we sh^d have no carpet when even the Taylor, Master Bond, hath one) and my ribbands and gown to be furbish'd, for 'twas decided that none but *Lucindy* sh^d have a new frock, so *I* had to go without, while she, pert minx, had a most loveley Gown of green callimanco, with Plumes to her hat. I wore my old tammie which is to thin for the seeson and has, more-by-token, been turn'd.

We were not, *this* time, so Forward in setting up the Night, as we were mightyly tyred, you may beleive. Come Morning 'twas clear, tho' somewhat Frosty, and good sister Anna minding to stay home & help Step-mother lay the table, Jonas & Edmund & I and the pert Lucindy, who is truley a great cross to me, set out for the Green. 'Twas tho't that M^r. Washington wo^d come by ten of the clock, but 'twas full noon ere he come. As he must enter by the road by the Parson's, I was for Walking out to meet him, but Jonas would not, wether from Sloth or from fear, I know not. Betimes M^r. Washington appered, bestridding a most hansome White horse. He wore a millitary Habit, much like that of my Worthy Father, only gayer and with fine things, I mind not what they call 'em, on the showlders. His Hat he wore under his arm, and he bent himself to the one side and the other as he Passed. I promise you we huzzared stoutly, but he bowed not, only leaned, as one sh^d say, towards us. Beside him road the Honble Mr. Phillips, the Worshippfull President of the Sennate. Behind come the two Seccretar^s Major (or Col^o) Jackson & Mr. Tobbias Lear, & ahind all grined a Black man. Over against the Meeting House stood to meet M^r· Washington all the great men of the Town (exsepting my Father who could not be spar'd from the House) and them that was in the fight. There was the Selectmen Masters Hammond Reed, John Chandler, Amos Marrett and Joseph Smith, there was the Honble Mr. Simons of the General Court and there was old Mr. Bridge and Maj. John Bridge, Sarjent Brown with his cheek all scared, Nath. Farmer with his arm in a Sling, tho' 'twas well, years agone, well favored Master Chandler who has gone and marryed more's the pitty and is to be a Cap^n in the Millisha, many Harringtous & Smiths and Sundry others, not forgeting Prince Estabrook the Black man, who was being made ackwainted, tho' stiffly, with M^r· Washington his servents, who had come up with his Coach. And there in the Front was your Father and the Parson. Your dad w^d have held the Pres^t his stirup, but he w^d not permitt of it, & threw himself from the sadle with a Jump, for 'tis said he is wonderus stroug, tho' so old. Then was there some figetting, none knowing what 'twas fiting to do. But M^r· Washington let them not stand loug abbashed, for he said, "Where is Leftenent Tidd, who was next to Cap'n Parker?" and when they put Master Tidd forward, the President gave him a fine grasp of the hand, saying nought, however. Then took he respectfuly the Parson his Hand, saying, "Our distinguish'd and dear Friend the Honble Govener has told me much of his fearless Kinsman, Parson Clark." Then followed some Speach which I heard not, daring to venture no nearer than I was, being that I had an old Frock, and compeled to hold back Lucindy. Soon the whole Troupe betook themselves to the Spot where the Blood was spilled.

 M^r· Washington seemed somthing sollem at first, but soon waxed livlyer and asked many Questions, they told me, of the Fight. He would, moreover, see the Houses round about, and when he enterred M^r· Buckman his Tavern, I was in great figget 'till he come out, fearing lest M^r· Merriam who is but just approbbated as a taverner and knows nought about the Bisness, might entreat him into Eating *there*. At last it being close onto two of the clock, the hour set for the dining, we set out, the Pres^t and the rest riding and walking at the head, and the Coach and the Townsfolk taging after, huzzaring and waving kerchefs. 'Twas a pitty we gave him no set speach as 'twas did in many Towns no biger than ours, and your Father could have writ it exselent. When we come to the house there stood my Father and step-mother at the tap-room Door, Anna and the naybors skulking in the parlour. My Father looked grandly in his rejimentels and proud indeed was I of him as he led the way to the Dinner-room prepar'd for M^r. Washington in the upper room, looking towards your House. 'Twas arrang'd that my Step-mother dish the vittles in the kitch'n, yours should bring them to the stares (the short way, thou knows't, thro' the shop & the Tap-room) and then my Father sho^d serve them to the gests. 'Twas permited me to stand in the corner betwixt the windows, to give what help was needed. We had a right fine feast, I can tell you, and much of it; rosted Beef, a showlder of pork, Chickins, pyes, Puddings, Sylly-bubs, and, best of all, some fine young Pigens sent in by the Widow Mulliken. M^r. Washington would have none but plane things, however, saying, as my Father handed the others to him, *That is to good for me*. When the pigens, of which there was but few, were served, the Pres^t said *Are all these fine kickshores for my servents to?* My Father stamering that he had not tho't to give them Such, his Highness bade the dish of Squobs be divided in half that his *Black men*, forsooth, might have the same as him. During the dining he talked of little other than the Vilenes of the Roads, calling them as Blind and Ignorent as the directions of the Inhabittents. He had more to say than was seemly, to my thinking, of the Ladyes, how hansome he found them, their black Hair being to his liking. He was exceeding Frugall in his drinking, as well as in his Feeding, for he took but one Mug of beer and two glasses of wine during the whole meal. After the second Glass he rellated sundry Aneckdotes, but with such gravyty & slowness that none durst smile. He told us that M^r. Franklin having been much Vexed in England by the British complaneing that the *Yankees*, as they term us, took a wrong advanttage on the 19th of April, in firing from behind Stone-walls, the great phileosofer had retort'd " Were they not *two* sides to the Walls?" The only other Storey I mind his telling is of his having come to a Tavern where the Host was away and where they had to arowse the Mistress, she being in bed; on hearing that the President was below, seeking shelter, she would have nought to do with him, beleiving him to be but the President of the little Yale Colledge in Conn$^{t.}$ A most diverting Thing took place after this; M$^{r.}$ Washington, you must know, is much besstirred over Farming matters and had much to ask of the crops *et cetera*, and so talking, he turned to Mr. Marrett and asked if he tho't not that the hogs in N. E. have exseeding long legs; this well-nigh upsett the comp'y, for you must know that 'twas Mr. Marrett who, at the last town meeting, contend'd that the Hogs sh^d be impownded, &, more by token, he will soon be named for Hog-reave himself, being about to Marry. The mirth at this might have prov'd Unbecoming had not just then arose a great cracking and howling. We rushed to the Window and there in the butt'nwood Tree was Jonas, clinging to the fril of Lucindy's skirt, and she dangeling in mid-air. Before we could get out of the Room, one of the Black-men had climed the tree and caught Lucindy by the Neck like a Cat, and carryed her down. The silly child had led Jonas into climing the Tree with her to look in at the dinner-room Window, and a limb having snapped she wo^d, but for Jonas, have broke her neck. Her new frock was quite spoyled. After the meal my Father shew the comp'y the Massonic Hall over the shopp for M$^r.$ Washington is a mason, but, sayes my Father, a very lukewarm one, thro' Pollicy. ' The forwerd Lucindy had meanwhile been put into an apon to hyde the Rents in her frock, and now she pushed herself into the President his presense. He notised her, perforce, and the minx was thereat Bold enough to intreat him go with her to get Pares from the old button-pare tree in the Hollow. He indulgentley consent'd & she led him thither. He raised her in his arms that she might reach the Pares, and on letting her down, I cannot Sware to it, but I firmly beleive, that he gave her a Smack. She is quite to Old, to my thinking, for such foldy-rol. His Highness then stood for a while afore the House, admiring at the trees, himself the center of all Eyes. Spying something White behind the wall oposite, he querried what it might be, at wch we well-nighe burst with larffing, for, in truth, 'twas your Granney herself, who had crawled up with much ado, & who was now peeping, her Cap all a-wry, to see the Pres^t.

The Sun being now low, Mr Washington entered his carrige, and started off to-wards Watertown, having denied a Mug of Flip which my Father, with much pains, had prepar'd. Messiers Tobyas Lear and Jackson and the Black men did not say him nay, tho', I warrant you.

I have burned 3 Dips, which is sinfull, & have set up long beyond Bell-ringing to send you this, so now must I stop.

Your ever afectionate
SALLY.

Post-scriptum. The President payed no Heed to me, w^{ch}, indeed, I would not have alowed, as did Lucindy.

Post-scriptum 2. If thou have a new Shalloon for Madam Washington's Friday route, do not ackwaint me of it lest I die with covetting.

Song, "Star Spangled Banner," sung by Mrs. Holt.

PRESIDENT MERRIAM.—As you have already learned, in his tour Washington tarried at Andover and was the guest of Samuel Phillips, then lieutenant-governor, who accompanied him from Andover to Lexington. Governor Phillips was the founder of that venerable institution of learning familiar to us as Phillips Academy. Andover could have no more fitting representative at our table to-night than the able instructor and principal of that institution, who will, with his enlivening words and manner, interest you in historical reminiscenses of Washington's visit at Andover.

I have the pleasure of introducing to you Dr. C. F. P. Bancroft, Principal of Phillips Academy of Andover.

Mr. President, Ladies and Gentlemen,—I wish to state at the outset what most speakers reserve to the close of their remarks, that I appreciate very highly the kindness and courtesy of this society, and especially of its officers in inviting me to be present and to take some part in this celebration. There are many men in Andover, some of them eminent in historical and antiquarian lore, who could more fittingly respond for our ancient town; for we had our share in that memorable day, a century ago, which Washington divided between Haverhill where he slept the night before, Andover where he breakfasted and paid a visit of courtesy, Lexington where he visited the battlefield and dined, and Watertown where he supped and spent the night,— not to omit Bradford, Wilmington, and Billerica, through which he passed. Our share in the day was less than yours, but we have treasured up the memories of it. Captain Osgood and a company of horsemen had been sent from Andover at the instance of Judge Phillips to escort the General as he journeyed from Salem to Newburyport, and Judge Phillips had himself accompanied him after his visit in Andover to Lexington, where he went over the historic ground with him and dined with him at the Munroe Tavern, returning to Andover when Washington set forward for Watertown. The house where Washington took his early breakfast is still standing on the North Andover road, and is now the residence of one of our substantial citizens, Hon. Samuel B. Locke. The daughters relate that strangers often ask the privilege of entering the house made memorable by this visit. It was then known as the Abbot Tavern, and there Mr. Phillips and several other local dignitaries met the President, and were entertained with him. There is a pretty tradition that Washington asked the landlord's little daughter to mend his riding-glove, and that he sealed his approval of her skill by taking her upon his lap and kissing her, whereat Miss Priscilla was so elated that she refused to have her face washed for a whole week afterwards. This anecdote, coupled with a similar one in your own annals, seems to give historical precedent and warrant for General Sherman's habit of giving expressive salutations to the young ladies of our day.

After breakfast, Washington, accompanied by an increasing throng, moved westward past the South Church and the minister's house, where several of his kinsmen found their home while students in the academy, and up what is now School Street, then lined on both sides by forest, to the new and for the times very elegant mansion of Judge Phillips, a house most unfortunately destroyed by fire two years ago this present month. Here he spent a short time conversing with Madame Phillips and her childen and a few invited guests. It is said that the moment he left the house Madame Phillips tied a band of blue ribbon to the chair in which he had sat, and at his death, ten years afterwards, she replaced the ribbon with a piece of crape. Ribbon and crape disappeared long ago, but the chair is fortunately preserved in the library of the Theological Seminary, and with it another just like it. Accordingly, we invite visitors to sit first in one and then in the other, that they may be able to say positively that they have sat in Washington's seat.

After his call at the Mansion House, the President mounted his horse, and sat for a few moments on the green opposite, receiving the respectful homage of citizens, teachers and boys from the academy, and persons from the adjoining towns. He then rode slowly down the Wilmington road, past what is now Latin Commons, on his way to Lexington.

We have, then, the old Abbot Tavern, the site of the Mansion House, a chair, and a few traditions to keep alive the memory of Washington's visit. These is, besides, in the academy building a cast of Houdon's bust; and, on the 22d of February, now and then waggish boys have been known to decorate it with hatchets and branches of some neighboring cherry-tree. There is somewhere — I have lost trace of it — a portrait of Washington, possibly by Stuart, but, if not a Stuart, certainly a clever copy, which was sent by Thomas Lee of Virginia in the name of his son, a grand-nephew of Washington, as a present to John, the son of Samuel Phillips, in acknowledgment of the kindness young Lee had received in Mr. Phillips's family and the friendship between the two boys. I have always hoped that at some suitable time this portrait might return to Andover, and be preserved in the academy collection.

In this visit, Washington renewed his acquaintance with Judge Phillips, an acquaintance which began during the siege of Boston in 1775, Mr. Phillips being a member of the Provincial Congress, and repeatedly appointed on committees to confer with the commander of the forces. Mr. Phillips had been very active, too, in manufacturing, at Andover, gunpowder for the army, and in other ways had been brought to Washington's favorable notice. Previous to this visit, Washington's nephew, Howell Lewis, the son of his sister Betty, had been sent to Phillips Academy, and, after his visit, Augustine Washington, Bushrod Washington, George Corbin Washington, brothers, sons of Colonel William Augustine and Jane Washington, and double grand-nephews of Washington; Richard Henry Lee Washington and John Augustine Washington, sons of Corbin and Hannah (Lee) Washington, — *i. e.*, grand-nephews of Washington and grandchildren of Richard Henry Lee; Cassius Lee and Francis Lightfoot Lee, brothers, grandsons of Richard Henry Lee, and grand-nephews of Washington on the side of their mother, Mildred Washington. In all, eight of Washington's own immediate kindred were in the academy. There are letters concerning these boys from Washington to Judge Phillips, — letters now in the possession of Rev. Phillips Brooks, — which show how immediate was Washington's interest in the education of these boys.

We have heard this evening with what enthusiasm, with what

marks of affection and admiration Washington was greeted at every stage in his journey. It is not surprising. He had not only shown himself "first in war," but in the slow and difficult creation of the Constitution, and in the organization and installation of the new government, he had already become "first in peace and first in the hearts of his countrymen." More than this. I suppose that at this time he was the most distinguished man in the whole world. The baleful Corsican star had not yet risen to dazzle and appall mankind. In France and in England, his name was a household word. Wherever liberty stirred, his name was the watchword of freedom. The eyes of the whole civilized world had been turned upon that infant nation which had triumphed in the unequal struggle with Great Britain, and had entered so boldly on an untried experiment in government. To see this renowned general, this consummate statesman, this idol of the people, this father of his country, this first President, to hear his voice, to grasp his hand,—this was a great event for our fathers; and it is worthy to be celebrated by their children. Whether we regard the character of Washington or his achievements, his virtues or his career, we do well to follow the injunction of the eminent British statesman, Lord Brougham, and "let no occasion pass of commemorating this illustrious man."

Ode by the quartet, sung in Boston at Washington's reception, Nov. 5, 1789.

The PRESIDENT,— On the banks of the Potomac there is a shrine to which all Americans have made, or desire to make, a pilgrimage. An unpretentious tomb contains all that is left of the great and good man. There is with us one whose ancestors were prominent and efficient in the Revolutionary War. They nominally represent the four quarters of the globe,— Europeus, Asiaticus, Africus, and Americus. A descendant of one of these, to fame not unknown, some years ago made the pilgrimage to Mount Vernon, and obtained access to the premises under circumstances singular and interesting, who will give you his experience thirty years ago.

I introduce to you Dr. Hamlin, of Lexington.

MY VISIT TO MOUNT VERNON.
MAY, 1837.

I HAD some special reason in childhood and youth for having an almost religious adoration of Washington. Both my grandfathers, Faulkner and Hamlin, were with Washington, the former on Dorchester Heights, the latter at Yorktown. Grandfather Hamlin had two sons that fought through the long Revolutionary War. Africus, the eldest son, kept a minute diary, Boswell-like, of everything he knew, saw, or heard of Washington. Besides four Hamlins, there were twenty-eight Revolutionary soldiers among the first settlers of Waterford, Me., my native place; and they brought with them sons and brothers. I was born into the outskirts of the camps of the Revolution. The above-named journal was always in request among those old soldiers, and not less so among their sons. It was hopelessly lost full seventy years ago. Woe worth the day!

When I received my appointment as a missionary to Turkey, Feb. 4, 1837, I resolved to visit Washington and Mount Vernon, if I could possibly compass it. Fortunately, I had a commission which paid my expenses. I fell in with good company by the way, which introduced me beyond any expectation. I was in clover at once. When I inquired about visiting Mount Vernon, I was told, "The weekly Mount Vernon steamer went yesterday with its party; and you cannot go till next week Wednesday." It was impossible to wait; and, against the protestation of friends that it would be useless, and, if I could reach the place, I would not be admitted, for all visits were confined to that one day, unless very specially introduced, I resolved to try it. I would at least see the place from without, and visit the tomb. I took the steamer to Alexandria, and called there upon a college friend, Professor Packard of the Episcopal Seminary, of which he is now the dean. He discouraged my going. The walk would be too long and wearisome, and I would not be received by Mrs. Washington,* the ravages of visitors having compelled to great strictness. I resolved, however, to try my luck. After a rapid walk of seven miles, made nine by devia-

---

*Mrs. Jane Washington, wife of Mr. John A. Washington, nephew of Bushrod. Mr. Washington was absent at the time.

tions, I reached the gate of the grounds, and was positively refused admittance by the old janitor, a solid, well-built, white-haired, venerable, good-looking negro. "It is impossible, sah, without you give me a letter. If you give me a letter, I take it to Massa Washington, and receive her commands." I pleaded my case; I gave him an account of myself and the distance I had come from way down East, etc. "I be very sorry, sah. You go right back to Washington, and bring a good letter. Dat's what you'll do, and massa will receive you kindly."

I then said: "Take me to the tomb, at least. That will hurt nobody." "'Gainst my orders, sah. O Lord, if we let 'em in, dey'll carry off dis gate and all dese trees. Dey are all like savages." His talk was very amusing; but I finally gained a point on him by asking when that conservatory was burned, and if that great singed cactus was planted by Massa Washington himself. He declared it was. It may have been, for aught I know; but, if I had asked him anything else, it would have been of the great Massa Washington. He let me in just to touch the plant which Washington had touched. I declared to him I had not come to Mount Vernon in vain. I stood before the very plant the great Father of his Country had planted. He repeated his advice about a letter, and then he would take great pleasure to show me everything. "Oh, it's a letter you want," I said. "Well, I will give you a letter." So I tore a leaf from my note-book, wrote an appeal to Mrs. Washington, folded it up, and addressed it to her. Then we had a comical argument about that's being a letter, he denying, I affirming. Finally, I said: "Let Madame Washington decide. If she rejects it, I go right out of that gate. If she accepts it, you are all right." He yielded, but went to the house so slowly that I feared he would turn back. He went in, however; I waited in suspense. Soon he came out, his dark face all aglow, and motioned me to come in. He opened the door, and bowed me into the hall with all the grace and dignity of a servant of Washington.

Mrs. Washington met me half-way in the hall, gave me her hand, and with charming cordiality said it gave her pleasure to welcome one who had made so long a pilgrimage. I must be very weary with my long walk. She gave me Washington's leaf chair to rest in and in his library. I was almost bewildered by such hospitality. She inquired about my destined life abroad, and seemed interested in it. She showed me the key of the Bastile, "the chamber where the good man met his fate," and various gifts of value from foreign sources. She then sent a servant with me to the tomb, and told him to cut some ends of branches of the cedar. I entered on the way the old tomb, still partly arched over, and broke off a piece of decayed board of the box that had enclosed the casket. Thirty-seven years in the damp tomb had taken the life out of the wood, so that I broke it without difficulty. I surveyed the marble sarcophagus in the new tomb through the double iron grill, received the cedar branches, and returned to express my profound gratitude to Mrs. Washington. There was one thing more to complete that immortal day. Mrs. Washington had prepared a simple, abundant collation of cold meat, bread and butter, and a decanter of wine, and remarked that every article, including the chair placed for me, was in use by Washington himself; and the food and wine were products of Mount Vernon. This was "Southern hospitality?" It was more than that: it was Christian hospitality,— the hospitality of a refined and noble lady, who believed me truthful and honest, and entered directly, with true womanly feeling, into sympathy with the dusty youth,— an absolute stranger,— who considered as nothing his double walk between Alexandria and Mount Vernon for the love and reverence he cherished.

PRESIDENT MERRIAM.— The reputation of Washington even in the early part of his career, still more later as his achievements became known, extended to other countries; and eminent men have joined with us in their tribute of praise and of commendation of our Washington. We have with us tonight one who has travelled much, seen much, and who has an eminent faculty of obtaining access to persons of importance in their various countries, and from his personal contact with many European statesmen he is well qualified to tell you of the high appreciation in which Washington is held by the great men of England and of Europe.

I introduce the Rev. E. G. Porter, of Lexington.

ADDRESS OF EDWARD G. PORTER.

Mr. President, Ladies and Gentlemen,— It is a great pleasure to me, after so long an absence, to find our society in such a flourishing condition. I have read many of the papers which you have printed, and found them both entertaining and instructive. I trust you will be encouraged to go forward in this good work, and continue your researches in all matters relating to the history of our town.

Your committee have done well in providing for such an appropriate observance of the interesting occasion which brings us together. Is it not a cause for mutual congratulation that we live in a town which offers us from time to time something worthy of being celebrated?

I have been asked to say a few words upon the estimation in which Washington is held among foreigners. We are not surprised to learn that one so eminent in his own country should win the respect and admiration of other lands. This could hardly be otherwise in the case of Washington; for his qualities as a patriot, a soldier, and a statesman, were so commanding as to attract universal attention. This was true even in his own time, and in the mother country, where the cause he represented was anything but popular. Whatever opprobrium rested upon the cause, or upon some of its leaders, very little was ever heard in England against the name or the character of Washington. Even Lord North and his ministry abstained from pouring out the vials of their wrath upon him, knowing, as they did, his unimpeachable integrity and his chivalrous devotion to the land of his birth. The friends of America in Parliament were greatly strengthened in their position by the noble bearing and singular magnanimity of Washington in the many trying emergencies in which he was placed. Burke, Chatham, Fox, Erskine, Brougham, and other eloquent defenders of our cause, found in him those exalted and heroic traits which they could proudly point to as a source of strength to the colonial cause, and as qualities which no true Englishman could refuse to admire.

The influence of such an example went far to carry conviction to the minds of the people of England that the demands of America were not so unjust as at first was generally supposed. And, after the war, so rapid was the change of sentiment that few public men were left who ventured to denounce a government over which presided the man who had won golden opinions from all lovers of liberty the world over. This is evident from the writings of that period, and from the changed legislation of Great Britain, new reforms being soon demanded in accordance with the principles which this country had shown were not incompatible with the dignity of law or the preservation of order.

The English statesmen of our time have unanimously indorsed this verdict; and such leaders as Cobden, Bright, and Gladstone have repeatedly spoken in the highest terms, not only of Washington, personally, but of the patriots who were associated with him in the struggle for independence.

And the opinion of England has been the opinion of the continent of Europe. Kings and princes, diplomatists and statesmen, scholars and poets, have not failed to see that our chosen leader was worthy to lead. Their tributes to his greatness are all the more significant because the existing institutions of the Old World were hostile to the political doctrines maintained in the New; and the success of our arms was clearly understood to menace the arbitrary and despotic systems then so widely prevalent.

Our achievement of liberty became an inspiration to thousands,— first in France and afterwards in Germany, where at the time there seemed to be little hope of any change. The idea of human rights began to be discussed in secret clubs and among the students of the universities. Interdicted pamphlets and popular songs embodied the new hope, and prepared the way for those political upheavals which have followed, one after the other, until most European countries have now obtained a constitutional form of government.

There are many brilliant names among those who have been the recognized leaders in the great national movements of modern times. The world is paying increasing honors to such men as William of Orange, Cromwell, Hampden, Coligny, Cavour, Garibaldi, and Castellar. In this galaxy, Washington will ever have a place; and, judging both by what he was and by what he did, it will be a place second to none.

I am happy to tell you, my friends, that Asia is at last coming to know our history and to appreciate our position. Thousands of young men in the missionary colleges of Turkey, in the universities of India, and in the popular schools of Japan, are studying with eager delight the career of our Washington and his contemporaries, hoping from such models to introduce among the nations of the East those types of civilization which have become the chief ornament and glory of the West.

And Australia is sufficiently advanced on the road to independence to appreciate the stimulating influence of such a name as that which we honor to-day. I saw in several of her public buildings and private residences portraits and busts of Washington, as well as one of Franklin in the Sydney Art Gallery, and the Declaration of Independence, with Hancock's familiar signature, hanging in the Museum of Brisbane. Yes: you may be sure that, wherever liberty gets a foothold in the world, there our country will be honored, and there our Washington will be exalted to the highest pinnacle of fame.

But, Mr. President, I cannot indulge in these reflections any further, because I have here an original letter of some length, describing Washington's visit to Boston, which I think you will all be glad to hear. It was written by Joseph Barrell,* a well-known merchant of the time, and one of the committee of three appointed to wait upon the President at Worcester, and arrange for his reception at Cambridge and Boston. The letter was written to a brother-in-law, General Samuel B. Webb, a former private secretary and aide-de-camp to Washington who served with distinction in the war, and was one of the founders of the Society of the Cincinnati in 1783. He held the Bible when Washington took the oath of office at New York as the first President. His son, James Watson Webb, became eminent as a journalist and a diplomatist, and I might add as a duelist, and died in New York as late as 1884.

This letter came into my hands, with some others of that period, in a most unexpected way. I was lately visiting some friends in Morristown, N. J., where I became much interested in the fine old mansion known as the headquarters of General Washington during the winter of 1777. It is strikingly like the Longfellow house at Cambridge. Having within a few years become the property of a patriotic association in New Jersey, it receives an annual State appropriation for its maintenance, and, with the spacious grounds, is daily thrown open to the public. Many Revolutionary relics (two thousand, I was told) have been placed there on exhibition, including several articles of furniture that once belonged to Washington. In a large glass case in one of the rooms I noticed a handsome velvet coat and vest, described as having been worn by Joseph Barrell at the reception given to Washington at Boston in October, 1789. The president of the association, Mr. Roberts, kindly gave me the address of the owner, Miss Mary Barrell, a grand-daughter of the Boston merchant; and from her I have obtained this valuable letter, which I will now proceed to read:—

*Mr. Barrell afterward resided on the fine estate now occupied by the McLean Asylum at Somerville.

BOSTON, 1st Novem. 1789.

Dear Sam

For the last 10 days we have done nothing but prepare for, and enjoy the visit of the best of men. I am sure after this 'twill be needless to mention His Majesty the President who does in a wonderful manner unite all hearts in sincere respect. To give you a detail of our proceedings would be only repeating the accounts already published, but I am persuaded both Jackson and Lear[1] will inform you that every attention that was paid appeared to be, and I have no doubt was, the effusion of the heart.

I had the honor with Mr. Breck[2] and Dr. Eustis[3] to be appointed a committee from the Town to wait on the good man at Worcester, to make the arrangements for his entrance into town, and we were determined to go in taste, in a coach and 4 horses, (Breck's and mine) 2 postilions and a servant on horseback. We were received with that politeness and dignity which marks every action of that illustrious character. After settling our business we set off for Boston and arrived in 9 hours and a half and timely effectually to arrange the procession.

I am told that His Majesty was much pleased with the order and regularity of the procession, saying it could not have been better had a soldier been posted by every citizen to keep them in order.

I have had the further honor to dine with him in Fanuel Hall and at Governor Bowdoin's, who was so polite. . . .

We were honored at the Assembly by his presence. The Hall[4] was elegantly decorated. Behind His Majesty was hung my handsomest tapestry and before him, as a carpet, the other. He was seated on a settee with the Vice President[5] and Lt. Governor[6] and Governor Bowdoin. The ladies were very handsomely dressed, and every one strove, here as well as every where else, who should pay the most respect. We had a very pretty Desert for supper with 3 fine Cakes (one for each set). . . .

The next morning at 8 o'clock he left us attended by a number of gentlemen in carriages and on horseback. I had the honor with my worthy Parson,[7] to be the only carriage that was at his lodgings before he set off. We were there 10 minutes before 8, knowing that would do. The others came 10 minutes after, which we knew would not.

The ladies were most of them decorated at the Assembly with sashes and caps (Martha's was a cap and thought it brilliant,) with G. W. and various devices. . . . On those for Hetty[8] and my

---

1 The President's secretaries.

2 Samuel Breck, a wealthy citizen, who lived in a fine old mansion on the north corner of Tremont and Winter streets, where Earl Percy for a short time had his quarters at the beginning of the war. See "Recollections of Samuel Breck," edited by Mr. Scudder.

3 Dr. William Eustis, afterward governor of Massachusetts, died 1825, buried at Lexington.

4 Concert Hall on Court Street.   5 John Adams.

6 Samuel Adams.   7 James Freeman.

8 Miss Webb, sister of Sally, who married Mr. Barrell.

daughter Hanah* (who made her first appearance) were a tolerable good likeness of the man himself with the trophies of war under his feet and the olive branch of Peace in his hand. Above, Justice crowning him with a wreath of laurel, and the motto: "*Virtue rewarded.*" On one of the trophies the name Washington in gold letters.

His Majesty while here went to the manufactory of sail cloth, and was exceedingly pleased. The spinning of this manufactory is done by a number of girls who were dressed clean, and in general are likely. His Majesty made himself merry on this occasion, telling the overseer he believed they collected the prettiest girls in Boston.

The card manufactory he also visited, and as everything that promises advantage to America must be pleasing to our friend, there can be no doubt he was pleased. . . .

Sally, Hetty, Hanah and Mr. N. B. jun^r. who are present desire their love to you. We all should have been glad to have seen you the time His Majesty was here. . . . We are all sick with colds, which we term Washington colds,† owing in a great measure to the stops on the Neck. . . . I had rather have one of his virtues than all his colds collected, but I will compound if he is not indisposed himself.

Remember me to all enquiring friends, not forgetting Col^o. Smith in a particular manner.

                  I am your friend and bro.

                            JO. BARRELL.

S. B. WEBB Esq. N.Y.
    Fav. M^r. B. Joy.

Allow me, Mr. President, to refer to a few additional matters, which I am sure will be of interest to Lexington people. No one here has mentioned the fact that the Colonnade, which was erected at the west end of the Old State House for the reception of Washington, was designed by the Hon. William Dawes, who on the night of the 18th of April, 1775, brought to Lexington the news of the coming of the regulars. By a preconcerted arrangement, he rode out over the Neck while Revere came by Charlestown.

The quaint music which Mr. Holt and his singers have given us so well to-night was originally sung by a choir stationed on the Triumphal Arch which spanned the street opposite the Colonnade. The composer was Oliver Holden of Charlestown, who, four years later, wrote "Coronation," that magnificent tune which I have heard in scores of languages all round the globe. His grand-

---

* Eldest daughter of Mr. Barrell by a former marriage, afterward Mrs. Joy of Boston.

† When President Tyler visited Boston in 1843, an influenza became very prevalent and was known as the Tyler grip.

daughter, Mrs. Edward Tyler, has for three summers been a guest at this house. I shall in due time take pleasure in presenting to this society the book which I hold in my hand, as a gift from Mrs. Tyler. It is entitled "Funeral Music for 22d February: Sacred Dirges, Hymns and Anthems, Commemorative of the Death of General George Washington, the Guardian of his Country and the Friend of Man. An original Composition by a citizen of Massachusetts." This was Oliver Holden, although he was too modest to allow his name to appear. Dr. Bancroft has told us of the President's visit to Andover. At Haverhill the day previous, Washington took occasion to call upon Sheriff Bartlett, whose official services he had enjoyed on the journey. Sheriff Bartlett was the father of our late fellow-citizen Charles L. Bartlett and the grandfather of General William Francis Bartlett, whose bust adorns our Cary Library.

Thus we find in many ways that our connection with Washington's visit is made very close and real to us. While we are proud of our inheritance, let us be true to the obligations of citizenship which the memory of Washington has forever consecrated in the hearts of our countrymen.

Mr. President, I see on my right the Rev. Mr. Hussey, of Billerica. We must not forget that Washington passed through Billerica that same day, and I hope Mr. Hussey will be good enough to say a few words to us.

PRESIDENT MERRIAM.— I have been anticipated in an intention to call upon one of our neighbors who is our guest to-night, and who comes from an adjoining town through which Washington passed, whom I will call upon to address you in those eloquent words which he knows so well how to use.

I have the pleasure of introducing to you the Rev. C. C. Hussey, of Billerica.

ADDRESS OF REV. C. C. HUSSEY.

Mr. President and Friends,— My name not being on the list of speakers of the evening, I have sat without care, and given myself up to the enjoyment of others' words. Now my sense of security is suddenly, if courteously, invaded; and, almost entirely without preparation, I must say something in response to the call.

Let me, friends, put you at ease from the start, and at this late hour earn your gratitude by saying that I do not intend a speech.

I can do, and certainly wish to do as much as this,—express my obligation for the kindness by which I, an outsider, am here, enjoying one of the most pleasant and satisfactory occasions in which I ever shared.

And I am glad of the opportunity of giving utterance to a heartfelt appreciation of the work of the Lexington Historical Society, to which we are indebted for this interesting evening, as well as for very much that tends to the satisfaction and improvement of the entire community.

When I was called upon to speak, it was for the purpose, it was said, of my saying some word in behalf of your neighboring town, Billerica. Well, we have not much there, that I have knowledge of, that has an association with Washington or his visit here. Of Revolutionary reminiscences we have a few, which I will make go as far as I can, for a substitute. The house is standing, but little changed, from which went the first man who fell at the battle of Bunker Hill; also the house at which a company of volunteer militia stopped for breakfast, when hurrying to the help of Lexington, on the ever memorable 19th of April. And on the same farm the large iron kettle has stood until within a short time, in which powder was made for the local militia, in the time of the country's scarcity of ammunition.

A detachment from Billerica, it was, in part, at least, which met and helped to harass the retreating British, at Merriam's Corner in Concord.

A native born might tell of occurrences of more interest. One thing claimed my attention. Washington's diary tells of his going through Billerica, on his way from Andover to Lexington. He might have gone some other way, but he did not; and I take this to be a compliment to the place, at least to its natural position, which is scarcely excelled by that of any town in the Commonwealth. I wish to congratulate you on the privilege you enjoy of being only eight miles from Billerica.

It would be impossible for any of you, probably, to understand the thoughts and feelings with which, as a boy, in my island home, I used to hear or read in my school-books of the battle fought here on your common, the "Battle of Lexington," which then seemed to me a far-off, wonderful land. Born of a long line of Quaker ancestry, in a town where the society of Quakers, or Friends, so largely prevailed that their principles, including the prominent one of non-resistance, pervaded and largely ruled the whole community, I regarded, without reasoning about it, all warfare, defensive as well as offensive, as unchristian. The "Battle of Lexington," and quite innocently and unconsciously the people of Lexington, stood to me as quite other than saintly, not to say anything more expressive. Taught in life's great school, I came later to be reconstructed, and to learn more fully that all true success, national as personal, is attained only through struggle,— that strife and warrings are the price of greatness. Still later, I came into personal acquaintance with Lexington people. I found they were not sinners above others, and were altogether a respectable, peaceable, kindly disposed folk, if their ancestors were fighters,— noble, heroic fighters, some of them, giving up their lives for God and their country.

Yours, friends of the Lexington Historical Society, is a noble work. I want to pay my tribute to it this evening. There are times when to look back is to move forward ; and to ponder the people and the ways of a hundred years ago, as we have been doing so interestingly this evening, cannot but arouse and strengthen some of the noblest impulses of our humanity. To be put into contact, as we have been, with the life of days forever memorable, must stir us to "make our lives more sublime." The gains of our age and of our own country, yet young among the nations of the earth, we own with wonder and gratitude. The marvellous changes continually going on in the social, political, financial, and religious economy of our land, tell us that "the face of man is toward the light and the day." But it may not be amiss, living in such an era of progress, to consider that some things of value may be dropped in a rapid march, and for the time be left behind. In the men and the times on which our minds have dwelt there was a stability of character, a solidity and conscientiousness of purpose, which we of to-day do well to exalt in our regard, and cherish into vigorous life. Whatever he was whom we have met this evening to honor, or was not, he was a man of deep religious principle. This gave to his character its crowning excellence. It was the sentiment of duty, rising above all merely personal considerations, a conviction of right, and the service man owes the right that made him, and those who labored with him, in that grand historic period, strong to battle with banded error and crowned wrong, invincible and triumphant in the warfare they waged, steady and grounded, whatsoever waves of opposition or hate might roll around them.

> "Our fathers' toil our ease hath wrought:
> They sowed in tears, in joy we reap."

Comforts, refinements, blessings without number, have gathered around our path; but life's warfare is not o'er.

The battle-ground is different, to be sure, the foes we have to meet are changed, less tangible, less rough, fairer-speaking, and more hidden beneath a covering of worldly prosperity and easy, luxurious living; but the battle must go on still if we, or the nation, go on toward the highest and best. Still must the armor be kept bright, still the strongholds of our fathers resorted to, — unwavering loyalty to an inward sense of right, a willingness to suffer, if need require, for the right, and trust in the eternal God.

And so, friends, in the occupations of this evening, its social minglings, its eloquent words and fitting songs, which have yielded us so much enjoyment, and in the work which your society and like associations are doing, we will build our altars of memorial to the highest truth of national and personal life, to our country, and to the man whom we delight to honor; and, putting our dependence where our fathers placed theirs, we ourselves will move on to do our part of the work of time, and transmit unimpared, and possibly, by Divine help, improved, the inheritance the ages have bequeathed to us.

PRESIDENT MERRIAM. — I cannot allow the exercises of this occasion to close without calling attention to the magnificent floral piece on my right which is the design and gift of Mr. F. B. Hayes. The name of Washington is well worthy to be glorified in nature's most beautiful forms and colors.

Song by the company: "Washington": Pierpont's Ode.

Articles of historic interest on exhibition at the old Munroe Tavern Nov. 5, 1889, the one hundredth anniversary of Washington's visit to Lexington: —

PERTAINING TO WASHINGTON.

Chair, pewter plate, cup, silver spoon, used by Washington at dinner Nov. 5, 1789.

Engraving from Stuart's portrait of Washington by Marshall, loaned by Mr. H. S. Gookin.

Engraving from a portrait of Washington by Schnessele, loaned by Mr. E. G. Champney.

Engraving from a portrait of Washington by (?), loaned by Mrs. Ellen Stone.

Certificate of membership in Society of the Cincinnati of Governor Eustis, signed by Washington, loaned by Dr. G. W. Porter.

Leaf from the tomb of Washington, loaned by Mrs. Ellen Stone.

Printed hankerchief in commemoration of Washington's resignation from the Presidency, loaned by Mrs. Ellen Stone.

Memorial engraving, "Sacred to the Memory of the Illustrious G. Washington," printed in 1801.

Personal letters of Washington, 1 vol., 8vo, loaned by Mrs. Ellen Stone.

Funeral sermon preached in Newburyport upon the death of Washington, loaned by Mrs. Ellen Stone.

Washington memorial pitcher, loaned by Mrs. Francis Wyman.

PERTAINING TO THE 19TH OF APRIL, 1775.

Sign of the old tavern "Entertainment by William Munroe."

Bullet-hole made in the ceiling of the bar-room by the musket of a British soldier.

Mahogany table used by British soldiers in making bonfire in the bar-room, with the purpose of burning the tavern, loaned by Mrs. Meserve.

Bar-room chair, used for same purpose, loaned by Miss L. M. Brigham.

ARTICLES IN THE TAVERN AT THE TIME OF WASHINGTON'S VISIT.

Wedding ring of Anna Smith, first wife of Colonel Munroe, 1767.

Wedding slipper of Anna Smith, first wife of Colonel Munroe.

Wedding furniture of William and Anna Munroe, 1767.

Round mahogany table, two arm-chairs, looking-glass, hat-tree, brittannia teapot, silver table-spoon (marked W. A.), loaned by Miss L. M. Brigham.

Spinning-wheel.

Rush-bottom chair.

Pewter candlestick.

Copper sauce-pan.
Iron fire-dogs.
Warming-pan.
"Loggerheads," for making flip.
Lemon-squeezer, for making punch.
Block used during the Revolution for stamping fabrics.

OTHER ARTICLES.

Masonic punch-bowl presented to Colonel William Munroe by the Hiram Lodge.

Map of the United States in 1792, loaned by Mrs. Ellen Stone.

Printed hankerchief showing plan of city of Washington early in this century, loaned by Mrs. Stone.

Photograph of the Washington monument with a piece of the stone, loaned by Mrs. Stone.

Two books printed in the last century, loaned by Mr. George W. Robinson.

Old vouchers, etc., from town records, loaned by Rev. C. A. Staples.

Bill of sale of a slave woman called Betty for £100 to Isaac Stone, of Lexington, 1743.

Printed handkerchief, fac-simile of the Declaration of Independence, loaned by Mrs. Francis Wyman.

Glass mug over two hundred years old, loaned by Mrs. Francis Wyman.

Silhouette (by King) of Miss Wyman, loaned by Mrs. Francis Wyman.

Photograph of Mr. Francis Wyman (born 1789), loaned by Mrs. Francis Wyman.

Portrait of Colonel William Munroe, by Greenwood; portrait of Jonas Munroe, by Pope; portrait of William H. Munroe, by E. G. Champney; photographs of Jonas, James S., William R., and Robert G. Munroe (five generations).

Walking-stick, military breeches, and iron spectacles belonging to Colonel William Munroe.

Baptismal shoe of William Munroe's second wife (Polly Rogers), 1756.

Child's stocking, belonging to William Munroe's second wife.

Silhouettes (by King) of William Munroe and Anna, his first wife.

Embroidered slippers belonging to one of the wives of William Munroe.

Bill of Rev. Timothy Minot against the town of Lexington for eighteen days' preaching in 1754

DECEMBER 10, 1889.

Regular meeting. President Merriam in the chair.

The following articles were presented to the Society : —

Two small English coins found at the Hancock-Clark House presented by Mr. Rumwell.

A copy of Biographical Memoirs of the illustrious General George Washington.

Several papers relating to Rev. Jonas Clark.

A petition to the selectmen, dated 1744.

The historian made a detailed report of the celebration of the Washington anniversary.

The following papers were presented : —

"The Early Schools of Lexington," by Alonzo E. Locke.

"Dorothy Quincy," by Ralph E. Lane."

www.ingramcontent.com/pod-product-compliance
Lightning Source LLC
Chambersburg PA
CBHW020242170426
43202CB00008B/187